THE BOLÍVARIAN REVOLUTION

This essential new series features classic texts by key figures that took centre stage during a period of insurrection. Each book is introduced by a major contemporary radical writer who shows how these incendiary words still have the power to inspire, to provoke and maybe to ignite new revolutions . . .

Also available:

Peter Linebaugh presents Thomas Paine:
Common Sense, Rights of Man and Agrarian Justice

Dr Jean-Bertrand Aristide presents Toussaint L'Ouverture:
The Haitian Revolution

Slavoj Žižek presents Trotsky:
Terrorism and Communism

Michael Hardt presents Thomas Jefferson:
The Declaration of Independence

Slavoj Žižek presents Mao:
On Practice and Contradiction

Walden Bello presents Ho Chi Minh:
Down with Colonialism!

Alain Badiou presents Marx:
The Civil War in France

Tariq Ali presents Castro:
The Declarations of Havana

Slavoj Žižek presents Robespierre:
Virtue and Terror

Terry Eagleton presents Jesus Christ:
The Gospels

Geoffrey Robertson presents The Levellers:
The Putney Debates

THE BOLÍVARIAN REVOLUTION

SIMÓN BOLÍVAR

INTRODUCTION BY HUGO CHÁVEZ

EDITED BY
MATTHEW BROWN

VERSO

London • New York

Verso
UK: 6 Meard Street, London W1F 0EG
US: 20 Jay Street, Suite 1010, Brooklyn, NY 11201
www.versobooks.com

ISBN: 978-1-84467-381-0

British Library Cataloguing in Publication Data
A catalogue record for this book is available from the British Library

Library of Congress Cataloging-in-Publication Data
A catalog record for this book is available from the Library of Congress

Typeset in Bembo by Hewer Text UK Ltd, Edinburgh
Printed in the US by Maple Vail

CONTENTS

Part III: Internationalizing the Revolution

INTRODUCTION

Hugo Chávez

On 15 August 1805, a young man climbed the Monte Sacro near Rome and made a solemn oath which was to have tremendous consequences for the course of world history.[1] "I swear by the God of my fathers," he said, "I swear on their graves, I swear by my Country that I will not rest body or soul until I have broken the chains binding us to the will of Spanish might!" Within two decades, the Spanish empire in the Americas had crumbled, and a chain of independent republics stretched from the River Plate to the mouths of the Orinoco, from Tierra del Fuego to the deserts of Mexico. Their liberation from colonialism was the outcome of a long struggle, involving countless thousands of men pitched into one dramatic battle after another. But to a large extent, the Americas owe their freedom to the burning energies, the intelligence and vision of one man: Simón Bolívar.

The Venezuelan writer Augusto Mijares once said that while Simón Bolívar was born in Caracas on 24 July 1783, *El Libertador* was born in Rome, on that August day in 1805. But who was the young man of 22 who made that impassioned, fateful promise? For one, he had been forged in the fires of suffering as a boy. The youngest of five children from the marriage of Juan Vicente Bolívar and María Concepción Palacios, he had been born into one of the richest families in the Spanish Americas—

the Bolívars owned *haciendas*, mines and slaves, and had business interests not only in Venezuela but across the Caribbean. But young Simón's life was not carefree—he lost his father at the age of three and his mother at the age of nine. Subsequently placed under the care of his maternal uncle, Esteban Palacios—a stern, strict man—the unhappy Simón ran away in 1795 to the house of his elder sister. The Caracas archives for the late 18th century record a case before the Royal *Audiencia*, which ruled that the Bolívar boy be taken from his sister's house—by force if necessary. In the end, the door had to be broken in, and Simón was dragged away kicking and screaming for all Caracas to see.

So Bolívar was also forged in the fires of rebellion. He would ride through the streets of Caracas, talking to boys from backgrounds very different from his own. In his tutor, Simón Rodríguez, he found a kindred spirit—a free-thinking philosopher and man of the Enlightenment who was to have a tremendous influence on Bolívar. Part of a group of dissidents conspiring against the Spanish Empire, Rodríguez was also a revolutionary. In 1797, after the conspiracy had been uncovered and its principal leaders executed, Rodríguez left Caracas and went into exile in the United States and Europe, having changed his name to Samuel Robinson. The young Bolívar, meanwhile, was sent to Madrid in 1799 to continue his studies, and though he wasn't what you would call a dedicated student, he did become a good rider and swordsman. In 1802, Bolívar married a young *Madrileña*, María Teresa Rodríguez del Toro, with whom he had fallen in love, and that summer they returned to Venezuela, to the family's estate in San Mateo, where Bolívar planned to take over the *hacienda*'s operations. But María Teresa died a few months later, leaving Bolívar widowed at 20 and plunging him once more into the fires of suffering.

Years later, Bolívar would say that if his wife had not died, he surely would have gone no further than becoming mayor of San Mateo. As it was, he returned to Madrid and took up a dissipated lifestyle, having affairs, going to many balls—and dancing well, by all accounts. But he was not just a man-about-town. He had read all the classics of the Enlightenment—Rousseau, Voltaire, Montesquieu—as well as many works on classical history and political thought. And he had arrived to a continent bubbling with political ideas, where Napoleon Bonaparte's star shone throughout. When Napoleon crowned himself Emperor in 1804, Bolívar was in Paris but was nearly expelled soon after for calling the Emperor a tyrant and a hypocrite in public. By the time he reached Rome in August 1805, the young Bolívar had been steeped in the ferment that was then traversing all of Europe. Here, having met once more with his old teacher Simón Rodríguez, he ascended the Monte Sacro to make his famous oath. Bolívar underwent a transfiguration: the young libertine, dancer and party-goer became *El Libertador.*

Simón Rodríguez used to say that the men who illuminate humanity's horizons are not born when they see the light, but when they begin to radiate their own. This is why we can say that the Liberator was born on the Monte Sacro in 1805. He spent the next twenty years ensuring that he fulfilled his oath, replacing the awful realities of colonialism with a new project that would take shape in the years of struggle ahead.

In 1807, Bolívar returned to his *hacienda* in Venezuela. But the world was changing. The Spanish Empire was beginning to lose its grip on its American colonies; Napoleon conquered Spain one year later and put his brother on the throne. While the war raged in the Iberian Peninsula, there was a crisis in the colonies. As the *criollo* elite in Caracas debated whether to stay loyal to the deposed Spanish king, Bolívar took a strong stand for full independence. On 4 July 1811, he told the deputies to a new national congress: "Let us banish fear and lay the foundation stone of American liberty. To hesitate is to perish." Independence was declared the very next day, and the First Republic was born.

But liberation did not succeed at the first attempt. The republic was defeated by Spanish royalist troops, who had convinced many slaves to ally with them against the *caraqueño* leaders of the republic. In March 1812 a terrible earthquake struck Caracas, killing thousands, which reactionary forces took as a sign that even nature was against the patriots. Within a few months, the Spanish army had cornered Bolívar, forcing him to leave Venezuela. At Cartagena, in what was then New Granada, Bolívar found refuge and wrote the "Cartagena Manifesto," where he analysed the reasons for the First Republic's defeat and called for New Granada and Venezuela to join together in the anti-Spanish struggle. "I believe that, unless we centralize our American governments, our enemies will gain every advantage," he wrote. Bolívar now took command of the patriots' cause, and following the "Admirable Campaign" of 1813, he returned to Caracas victorious and established the Second Republic.

But it too was short-lived. In 1814, a rebellion of slaves and the poor defeated the troops of the Second Republic and Bolívar went into exile once more—this time to Jamaica, where many refugees from Venezuela and New Granada had come fleeing persecution by the Spanish Empire, and where he passed the next seven months from May to December of 1815. Bolívar, now very much the leader of a revolution, tried to rally support for his cause from the British government but was unsuccessful—as his fellow Venezuelan and leading patriot, Francisco de Miranda, had also been in his attempt to gain the backing of the French. Europe was more monarchical than ever, and its crowned heads had much to fear from movements built around slogans of liberty and equality.

These were months in which Bolívar thought a great deal, as can be seen in his letters and writings from the period, the most significant of which was the "Jamaica Letter." If *El Libertador* was born in 1805, we could also say that it was in Jamaica in 1815 that the Bolívarian project of integration was born.

It was here that Bolívar's unitary geopolitical vision surfaced and that his project was forcefully laid out—a project that was continental, anti-imperialist, republican, egalitarian and libertarian, and one he would work to carry out in the years to come. The wisdom of his analysis is impressive, particularly since he was only 32 at the time. He carries out a diagnosis of almost every country in the Americas, stretching from Mexico to Buenos Aires. "Let us cast our eyes around, and we shall see, throughout the whole extent of this immense hemisphere, a simultaneous struggle," he writes. "Do we not see the whole of this new world in motion, armed in our defense?" Then he looks deep into the past, comparing the situation of the Americas with that of other peoples and seeing the passivity of a continent trapped for years under Spanish domination— which provides more fuel for his anger: "It is an outrage and a violation of the rights of humanity to pretend that a people so blessed by nature, so extensive, rich, and populous, should be merely passive."

In this text, Bolívar also declares himself anti-monarchist:

American monarchies are less useful. I will give my reasons. The interest of a republic, when well understood, is confined to preservation, prosperity, and glory. Republic liberty is precisely the opposite of dominion. There is no stimulus to excite republicans to sacrifice their means to extend their boundaries . . .

And he then goes even further:

when a state becomes too extensive, either in itself or from its dependencies, it falls into confusion, converts its free form into a sort of tyranny, abandons those principles which ought to preserve it, and at length degenerates into despotism. The essence of small republics is *permanency*, that of great ones is *changeability*, but always inclined to dominion.

We can see here that Bolívar was an anti-imperialist—the first anti-imperialist in the history of the Americas.

At the beginning of 1816, Bolívar went to Haiti, which had been freed from the French by the revolution of the 'black Jacobins', as C.L.R. James called them. Bolívar was preparing an expedition to Venezuela to carry on the struggle for Liberation. The president of Haiti, Alexandre Pétion, gave Bolívar more than moral support—he provided guns, boats, supplies and money in exchange for a promise to free the slaves in all the territories Bolívar liberated. Bolívar had understood that independence would not be possible without the participation of the Venezuelan people—the poor, the *peones*, the slaves and the blacks. The first thing he did when he disembarked was to order the emancipation of the slaves and social equality for all, through a celebrated decree signed in Carúpano on 2 June 1816:

> Considering that justice, policy, and the country imperiously demand the inalienable rights of nature, I have decided to formally decree absolute freedom for the slaves who have groaned under the Spanish yoke during the three previous centuries.

But despite this, the slaves were not fully freed until much later: the slave-owners and oligarchs all opposed Bolívar's egalitarian social vision. When he died in 1830, it was to the sound of slaves singing at midday at the *hacienda* San Pedro Alejandrino. It is said that he sighed and said: "It smells of San Mateo," remembering his family's own *hacienda*, in the days before he brought freedom to the continent.

★　　★　　★

Bolívar's expedition of 1816 was defeated, but he was not deterred; he regrouped in Haiti once more, and this time, in April 1817, sailed further up the coast to the delta of the Orinoco River. Moving up the river, he established his base at Angostura—now named Ciudad Bolívar in his honour—and forged an alliance with José Antonio Páez, leader of the *llaneros*, the men of Venezuela's plains. For two years, the forces of liberation fought for control of the Orinoco basin and the plains. In February 1819 a new Venezuelan Congress met, where Bolívar gave the speech now known as the "Angostura Address." Here he laid out his vision of the ideal political system for the Americas, based on the principle that "the most perfect system of government is that which produces the greatest degree of happiness, of social security, and political stability." And we can see here again the importance he placed on emancipating the slaves: "I leave to your sovereign authority the reform or repeal of all my ordnances, statutes, and decrees, but I implore you to confirm the complete emancipation of the slaves, as I would beg my life, or the salvation of the Republic."

The years that followed were crowned with one brilliant military success after another as the tide of liberation became unstoppable. In mid-1819, Bolívar led his army in a heroic crossing of the Andes and resoundingly defeated the Spanish at Boyacá: New Granada was now free. In 1821, victory at Carabobo cleared the way to Caracas, and Bolívar entered in triumph on 29 June—Venezuela too was now independent. Ecuador followed in 1822—Bolívar rode into Quito in June. Only Peru remained, and in September 1823 Bolívar set out for the port of Callao to take charge of the independence struggle there. He scored a crucial victory at Junín in the highlands in August 1824, but the final moment of glory came at year's end at Ayacucho, where defeat for royalist forces meant the wars for independence were effectively over. The Americas had been liberated, and Bolívar had fulfilled the promise he had made in Rome two decades before. In 1825, the territory of Upper Peru was renamed Bolivia in recognition of his staggering achievement.

Bolívar was a true revolutionary. He became more revolutionary each day as he advanced in his struggle across South America, pushing for the liberation of slaves; confiscating land and distributing it among the indigenous people; setting up schools, including ones for girls, indigenous children and the children of slaves. Barely a month after the Battle of Boyacá, for example, a decree on education in the *Gaceta de Santa Fe de Bogotá* on 10 October 1819 specified that children should be taught to read and write, along with the basic principles of grammar, of religion and morality, drawing, logic, mathematics, physics, geography, and engineering—for the construction of roads and housing. Here is a man who defeated the empire with his sword but thought as well about the future of the people he was liberating. Military actions were meant to pave the way for social revolution. We can see it again in a decree he made in Chuquisaca (today the city of Sucre) on 14 December 1825 regarding agriculture, which ordered a redistribution of land. "Every individual, whatever their sex or age, will receive one *fanegada* [44 hectares] of land." Here Bolívar is establishing a principle contrary to those of capitalism: a socialist principle. Every day, in fact, I become more convinced that the evolution of Bolívar's thought pointed toward socialism. If he had lived a few decades longer, I am absolutely sure he would have become a socialist, much like his teacher Simón Rodríguez.

Even as he was liberating Peru, Bolívar was thinking about how best to guarantee the freedom of the new republics. In his precocious maturity and with the wisdom he had acquired on the battlefield and in his political battles, Bolívar foresaw the difficulties that lay ahead: "If America does not call itself to order and reason there will be very little guarantee of the stability of the newborn governments, and we will bequeath to posterity a new colonial status." He proposed a union of republics stretching from the Caribbean to Patagonia, and in December 1824 invited all the South American leaders of his time—Bernardo O'Higgins, José de San Martín, José Abreu e Lima, José Artigas—to a congress in Panama. Though it was eventually held in 1826, it was a failure: the unity that Bolívar called for never arrived. Instead, the rising power of the United States imposed itself—it was around this time that James Monroe in Washington came up with his Doctrine about Latin America being the backyard of the US. And that is how it has been ever since. I often ask myself, where would Latin America be today—how different would its social, economic and political reality be?—if US imperial power had not trampled the progressive governments that arose in these lands?

Bolívar foresaw the threat of the US and described it with surprising clarity: "the United States seems destined by Providence to plague America with miseries in the name of Freedom." He continues: "There in the North, at the head of this continent, is a very large nation, very hostile and capable of anything." On another occasion he asked: "What kind of brothers are these, those in North America, when even Spain has now recognized our independence and they still refuse to do so?" But Bolívar's anti-imperialism was just one part of his great overall vision. He wanted equality, liberty and a union of republics to achieve a multi-polar world, ideas that continue to resonate powerfully today. His call for unity in Latin America especially should serve as a beacon. None of the countries of the continent are individually strong enough to make powerful strides forward and achieve a greater degree of independence on their own—in fact, this is perhaps truer today than it was two hundred years ago.

★   ★   ★

Following Bolívar's years of triumph came five years of tragedy, as the continent he had liberated fell into the hands of local oligarchies. Between 1825 and 1830, Bolívar's project shattered into countless pieces, broken by opposition from wealthy landowners, and under pressure from the first wave of North American imperialism. Bolívar died in Santa Marta on the Caribbean coast of Colombia on 17 December 1830, at the age of 47. Though he had been born rich, he died without any material wealth of his own—his body had to be dressed in a borrowed shirt because the one he was wearing when he died was tattered. He had been abandoned by everyone, and died comparing himself to Don Quixote: "I have ploughed the sea."

But Bolívar's project did not die with him. "I awake every hundred years when the people awake," as *El Libertador* says in a poem by the great Pablo Neruda. The Venezuelan people have once again taken up that project, and with them the peoples of Latin America and of the world. They are waging a new struggle for a world of equals, a world of justice. The better world we want to construct is no longer only possible but absolutely essential. Things cannot continue as they are: either we change the world or it will end. This is something I am sure Bolívar would have understood, since he was always thinking of the destiny of the Americas and the world in the centuries to come. His project was always oriented toward the future. It was not possible then—but the future is now. There is no time to lose!

NOTE

1 This introduction has been compiled and edited from the speeches of Hugo Chávez.

FURTHER READING

Due to the vast number of works published on Bolívar, this list has been limited to works in English only. The bibliographies of the works listed below provide an introduction to the even more voluminous literature in Spanish and other languages.

BIOGRAPHIES

Lynch, John, *Simón Bolívar: A Life* (New Haven: Yale University Press, 2006)

Bushnell, David, *Simón Bolívar: Liberation and Disappointment* (New York: Pearson, 2004)

BOLÍVAR'S WRITINGS

Bushnell, David, ed., *El Libertador: Writings of Simón Bolívar* (Oxford: Oxford University Press, 2003)

Bierck, Harold, and Vicente Lecuna, eds., *Selected Writings of Simón Bolívar* (New York: Sociedad Bolivariana de Venezuela, 1951), 2 vols.

STUDIES ON BOLÍVAR AND INDEPENDENCE

Brown, Matthew, *Adventuring Through Spanish Colonies: Simón Bolívar, Foreign Mercenaries and the Birth of New Nations* (Liverpool: Liverpool University Press, 2006)

Conway, Christopher Brian, *The Cult of Bolívar in Latin American Literature* (Gainesville: University of Florida Press, 2003)

Davies, Catherine, Claire Brewster and Hillary Owen, *South American Independence: Gender, Politics, Text* (Liverpool: Liverpool University Press, 2006)

Earle, Rebecca, *Spain and the Independence of Colombia* (Exeter: University of Exeter Press, 2000)

Lynch, John, *Latin American Revolutions 1808-1826* (Norman: University of Oklahoma Press, 1994)

Murray, Pamela, *For Glory and Bolívar: The Remarkable Life of Manuela Sáenz* (Austin: University of Texas Press, 2008)

CHRONOLOGY

1783
24 July: Simón José Antonio de la Santísima Trinidad
                        Bolívar y Palacios born in Caracas.

1799–1802   Bolívar visits and lives in New Spain (Mexico),
                        Spain and France.

1802
26 May: Bolívar marries María Teresa Rodríguez del
                        Toro in Madrid.

1803
22 January: María Teresa Rodríguez del Toro dies in
                        Caracas.

1803–1807   Bolívar travels to Spain, France, Italy and the
                        USA.

1810
19 April: Caracas rebels against colonial rule and
                        deposes Captain-General. New *junta* governs,
                        autonomously, in the name of deposed King
                        Fernando VII.
                        Bolívar travels to London as part of Venezuelan
                        mission seeking recognition of its independence
                        (returns to Venezuela in December).

1811

5 July: Elected Venezuelan Congress declares
                           independence. Beginning of First Republic.

1812

26 March: Earthquake in Caracas.
6 July: Bolívar abandons Puerto Cabello.
31 July: Bolívar complicit in arrest of Francisco de Miranda.
                           End of First Republic. Bolívar seeks asylum in
                           New Granada.
15 December: Bolívar issues Cartagena Manifesto.

1813   Bolívar's Admirable Campaign, beginning of
                           Second Republic.

1814   End of Second Republic, defeated by Spanish
                           Reconquest under Monteverde and Boves.

1815   Reconquest of New Granada. Bolívar goes into
                           exile in Jamaica.
6 September: Bolívar publishes "The Jamaica Letter".

1816   Bolívar moves to Haiti to prepare an attack on
                           Venezuela.
                           Leads Los Cayos Expedition from Haiti to
                           Venezuela.
2 June: Bolívar publishes decree against slavery in
                           Carúpano.
1817–18   Bolívar consolidates power in Orinoco basin
                           with government in Angostura.

1819

15 February: Inauguration of the Congress of Angostura.
25 July: Battle of Pantano de Vargas.
7 August: Battle of Boyacá.
10 August: Bolívar enters Bogotá.
25 November: Six-month armistice signed with Spanish Army
                           Commander General Pablo Morillo.
17 December: Congress of Angostura votes to establish
                           Republic of Colombia.

1821   Colombian Constituent Congress meets at
                         Cúcuta.
                         Bolívar elected President and Francisco de Paula
                         Santander as Vice-President.
24 June: Battle of Carabobo.

1822
24 May: Battle of Pichincha.
26–27 July: "Guayaquil Interview" between Bolívar and San
                         Martín.

1823
1 September: Bolívar arrives in Peru and assumes leadership of
                         wars of independence.

1824
6 August: Battle of Junín.
7 December: Bolívar invites Spanish American nations to
                         Congress of Panama.
9 December: Battle of Ayacucho.

1825   Upper Peru falls to Sucre's armies.
                         Bolívar invited to write constitution for Republic
                         of Bolivia.

1826
25 May: Bolívar presents his draft Constitution to the new
                         Republic of Bolivia.
April–September: La Cosiata rebellion in Venezuela.
3 September: Bolívar leaves Peru for Colombia.

1828   Ocaña Convention.
25 September: Assassination attempt on Bolívar in Bogotá.
Late September: Execution of conspirators, including José Padilla.

1829   Rumours of monarchy project (with plans to
                         crown Bolívar, or an imported European prince)
                         spread across Colombia.
September: Bolívar's loyal general José María Córdova rebels
                         against him.

| 17 October: | Córdova defeated at Battle of El Santuario, Antioquia. |

1830

1 May:	Bolívar resigns Presidency.
8 May:	Bolívar leaves Bogotá intending to go into exile.
17 December:	Bolívar dies in Santa Marta.

1830–31   Disintegration of Gran Colombia into the separate republics of Venezuela, Ecuador and New Granada (known as Colombia since 1863).

GLOSSARY

Alcalde: District magistrate or mayor.

Casta: Various people of mixed racial heritage in colonial Latin America, generally applied (as *las castas*) to all non-white peoples.

Caudillo: Leader whose rule is based on personal power rather than on constitutional form.

Congress of Angostura: Legislative Assembly which met to govern the Republic of Colombia 1819-21.

Congress of Cúcuta: Constituent Assembly which met in Cúcuta (close to the New Granada–Venezuela border) to govern the Republic of Colombia in 1821 (when the capital was formally moved to Bogotá) and which discussed and approved the 1821 Constitution of Cúcuta for a ten-year period.

Convention of Ocaña: Constituent Assembly which met in Ocaña (in northern New Granada) in 1828 to revise the Cúcuta Constitution, which it failed to do because of disagreements between the followers of Bolívar and Santander.

Cordillera: Mountain range, as in "Cordillera de los Andes".

Cosiata, La: Political rebellion in Venezuela, April–September 1826, in which centralized authority (and Bolívar's right to rule) was questioned and debated.

Creole: *Criollo*, generally a person of Spanish descent born in the Americas; Spanish American.

Cundinamarca: The region/province of Santa Fe de Bogotá in New Granada, with which it was sometimes equivalent at the time of independence.

Encomienda: Grant of indigenous labour initially awarded to the participants of the wars of conquest in the sixteenth century.

Gran Colombia: The Republic founded by Bolívar in 1819 consisting of the present-day territories of Venezuela, Colombia, Ecuador and Panama; it ceased to exist in 1831.

Hacienda: Colonial estate, owned by a *hacendado* such as Bolívar.

Independence: The removal of colonial authority from a land.

Llanos: Plains in the New Granadan and Venezuelan interior: *llaneros*, those who live and work upon them.

Mantuano: A member of the white Caracas landowning colonial elite, such as Bolívar.

Mestizo: In common usage, a person of mixed heritage, usually Indian/Spanish.

New Granada: The Viceroyalty of New Granada, with its capital at Santa Fe de Bogotá, existed until the last viceroy fled in 1819, just before Bolívar arrived. In 1831, after the disintegration of Gran Colombia, a Congress meeting in Bogotá chose to retake the name New Granada for their territory, which it retained until 1863, from when it has been known as Colombia.

New Spain: The Viceroyalty of New Spain, with its capital at Mexico City, included all of present-day Mexico and Central America with the exception of Panama (which pertained to New Granada/Colombia until its independence in 1902).

Pardo: Of mixed race, with African ancestry; free coloureds.

Pardocracia: Government by *pardos* (much feared by Bolívar).

Patria: Native land, mother country; literally fatherland.

Patria Boba: "Foolish Fatherland," term ascribed to First Venezuelan Republic 1811–12.

Pueblo: Village, town or people.

Reconquests: Successful Spanish attempts to regain control of Venezuela and New Granada in 1812–13 and again in 1815–16.

Resguardo: Reservation, land allocated to organized and sedentary indigenous peoples.

KEY FIGURES

Acosta (José de) 1539–1600: was a Jesuit naturalist and traveller, the author of *Historia natural y moral de las Indias* (1590).

Almagro (Diego de) c.1475–1538: was a Spanish conquistador in the conquests of Peru and Chile, also known as *El Adelantado.*.

Antoñanzas (Eusebio) 1770–1813: was a Spanish military officer famed for his harsh repression of civilians and military forces alike during the "reconquest" of 1812–13.

Atahualpa c.1497–1533: was the last sovereign emperor of the Inca Empire, executed in Cajamarca by the conquistadores under Francisco Pizarro

Blanco (José María) 1775–1841: was a Spanish liberal exiled in England, where he published widely in support of the movements for Spanish American independence. He was known in Britain as Joseph Blanco White; he died in Liverpool.

Bonaparte (Napoleon) 1769–1821: was the French General and Emperor whose invasion of the Iberian Peninsula in 1807 triggered the disintegration of the Spanish monarchy in the Americas.

Boves (José Tomás) 1782–1814: was an Asturian-born naval officer and businessman who arrived in Venezuela at the start of the 1800s. In 1812 he joined the Royalist "reconquest" of Venezuela in the *llanos*. He was Bolívar's most notorious enemy in the War to the Death, famed for his apparent bloodlust. He died in action.

Boyer (Jean-Pierre) 1776–1850: was President of Haiti from 1820–1843, born a free mulatto and veteran of the independence struggle against France.

Brión (Louis) 1782–1821: Curacao-born, Dutch-educated naval admiral and financier of the wars of independence who commanded Venezuela's navy until his death from tuberculosis.

Carlos IV 1748–1819: was Bourbon King of Spain from 1788 to 1808. His ministers, particularly Manuel Godoy, were the architects of the later Bourbon Reforms which catalyzed opposition to Spanish rule in many of the American colonies. He abdicated the throne in favour of his son Fernando VII, and died in exile in Rome.

Carnot (Lazare) 1753–1823: was a French revolutionary general and administrator.

Castel (Charles-Irene) 1658–1743: was a French writer and priest, also known as the Abbé de Saint-Pierre.

Cervéviz (Francisco Javier) *dates unknown:* was a Spanish officer renowned for acts of cruelty during the reconquest in 1812–14.

Chasseboeuf (Constantin-François) 1757–1820: the Count of Volney was a French scholar and liberal writer.

Columbus (Cristóbal Colón) 1451–1506: the Genoa-born navigator credited with the "discovery" of the Americas after the first of his four voyages in 1492.

Córdova (José María) 1799–1829: Antioquia-born General who led infantry charge at Battle of Ayacucho. He was a loyal Bolivarian throughout the 1820s until, angered by rumours that Bolívar wished to return to a form of monarchical rule for Colombia, he led an armed rebellion in his home province of Antioquia (New Granada), which was defeated. He died after the Battle of El Santuario.

Cortés (Hernán) 1485–1547: the Spanish conquistador who conquered the Aztec empire and founded New Spain.

Cristóbal (Henri-Christophe) 1767–1820: one of the leaders of Haitian independence who was crowned King and ruled as such from 1811 to his death.

Cuauhtemoc c.1502–1528: the Aztec emperor executed by Hernán Cortés.

Dessalines (Jean-Jacques) 1758–1806: the first ruler of independent Haiti, who was crowned Emperor in 1804 and ruled until his assassination.

Devereux (John) 1778–1860: was a member of the United Irishmen uprising suppressed by Britain in 1798. Between 1818 and 1821 he recruited and then led the 1,700 members of the Irish Legion who fought for Colombian independence.

Fernando VII (1784–1833): was officially King of Spain from 1808, when his father Carlos IV abdicated under pressure from Napoleon Bonaparte. Fernando was then himself replaced on the throne by José I, better known as Joseph Bonaparte, Napoleon's brother. For many moderate Spanish Americans, Fernando VII became *el deseado,* the desired one, whom they wished to return to the Spanish throne and restore their rights. When Fernando did return to the throne, in March 1814, he supported a hard-line policy with regard to the American colonies, which exacerbated the alienation of those Creoles who had longed for his return. He reigned until his death in 1833 and never accepted the loss of the American colonies.

Guerra (Fray Servando Teresa de Mier) 1763–1827: was a priest who argued for the independence of Mexico, more commonly referred to today as Servando de Mier.

von Humboldt (Alexander) 1769–1859: German explorer and scientist renowned in Bolívar's time for his travels and research across Hispanic America, and the subsequent publications.

Iturbide (Agustín de) 1783–1824: was the military officer who led the negotiated independence of Mexico from Spanish rule in 1821, and who served as Emperor of Mexico, Agustín I from 1822-23. He was executed on his return from exile.

Lafayette (Marquis de) 1757–1834: led the French support for the rebel cause in North America in 1777. He was a noble deputy in the Estates-General. He argued for conciliation between the French king and the Revolution and was later a support of constitutional monarchy in France.

Lara (Jacinto) 1777–1859: was a long-serving officer throughout the wars of independence who was promoted to General of Division after the Battle of Ayacucho.

Las Casas (Bartolomé de) 1484–1566: was a Dominican priest, the first Bishop of Chiapas, and a staunch defender of the rights of indigenous peoples in the Spanish Empire.

Manco Capac was the legendary founder of Inca civilization; he was the son of the sun god, Inti.

Miller (William) 1795–1861: was a British mercenary who served in the wars of independence in Chile and Peru, and was later Governor of Potosí.

Miranda (Francisco de) 1750–1816: was the great "precursor" of Venezuelan independence, living for many years in Europe and lobbying the great powers to intercede on his behalf. His practical attempts at liberation (principally with an army of US and British mercenaries in 1806) ended in failure. In 1812 his efforts to negotiate a settlement with strong Royalist forces led to some Patriots (including Bolívar) to arrest him and remove him from the resistance's leadership. He was subsequently captured by Royalists and spent three years in Spanish prisons before dying in gaol in Cádiz.

Miyares Pérez y Bernal (Fernando) 1749–1818: was a Cuban born colonial administrator who was Governor and Captain-General of Venezuela in 1810–1812 at the time of the first movements for independence.

Monteverde (Domingo de) 1773–1832: was a naval veteran of the Battle of Trafalgar (1805) who led the first wave of Spanish "reconquest" against Venezuelan independence in 1812 and 1813.

Montezuma c.1480–1520: was as Emperor Montezuma II the leader of the Aztecs at the time of the Spanish conquest; he died in captivity or in battle with Spanish forces.

Necochea (Mariano) 1792–1849: was an Argentine general who served under José de San Martín in the Chilean and Peruvian wars of independence.

Olmedo (José Joaquín) 1780–1847: was a Bolivarian loyalist and poet who served briefly as President of Ecuador in 1845.

Páez (José Antonio) 1790–1873: was a *llanero* fighter who rose to a position of popular and military hegemony in early independent Venezuela. He was President of Venezuela between 1830-34, 1839-43 and 1861-3, and died in exile in New York.

Pétion (Alexandre) 1770–1816: was President of Haiti from 1810 until his death, a free black who assisted Bolívar considerably during the Liberator's Haitian exile.

Piar (Manuel) 1774–1817: was a multi-lingual Curacao-born *pardo* naval officer who served the Haitian government before enlisting in Venezuela in 1810. He commanded forces in Venezuela during the time that Bolívar was in exile and was therefore the focus of opposition to Bolívar's assumption of leadership. His death represented the victory of the white *mantuano* elite in the leadership of the independence movements.

Pizarro (Francisco) 1476–1541: was the Spanish conquistador who led the conquest and initial colonization of Peru.

Pradt (Abbé Dominique de) 1759–1837: was a French priest and writer who became a staunch supporter of Bolívar and Spanish American independence.

Raynal (Abbé Guillaume Thomas) 1713–1796: was an influential French critic of Spanish colonialism.

Santander (Francisco de Paula) 1792–1840: was Vice-President of Colombia under Bolívar in the 1820s. Implicated in the assassination attempt on Bolívar in September 1828 he was sent into exile. He returned to serve as President of New Granada from 1833-7.

Sucre (Antonio José de) 1795–1830: was the Venezuelan General most trusted by Bolívar. He led the victorious independent armies at the Battle of Ayacucho, and was the first President of Bolivia. Widely believed to be Bolívar's heir apparent he was assassinated by political opponents in Berruecos in the south of Colombia.

Walton (William) 1784–1857: was a journalist and publicist who promoted Bolívar's cause in Britain.

NOTE ON THE TEXTS

One of the problems that English readers often find when they first encounter Bolívar's writings is the dense style of the existing translations which replicate the long sentences and proliferation of pronouns of the original Spanish. These translations are accurate to the tone and content of the original but on some occasions can make comprehension difficult for the uninitiated. Here, I have tried to make Bolívar's writings more accessible to contemporary readers who may be unacquainted with the style and phrasing of the early nineteenth century. For the longer "major" works, I have gone back to the first English translations which were published contemporaneously with the Spanish originals, and revised and updated them for present-day readers. In this way I hope to have kept as close as possible to Bolívar's original revolutionary messages as they were distributed internationally during his lifetime, while making them clear and readable today.

For Document 6, "The Jamaica Letter," I have revised and updated the original English translation, published in the *Jamaica Quarterly Journal and Literary Gazette* in July 1818. I decided to return to and revise the tone of this first English publication, in order to get close to the original meaning over which Bolívar himself had probably some influence. Though he was far from a fluent English speaker, Bolívar probably discussed the content with John Robertson, the supposed translator, at some length during his exile in Jamaica. The text differs in some ways from the version used by most historians, being slightly shorter, lacking some later editorial insertions and retaining some acerbic comments and clarity of expression.

For Document 10, the "Angostura Address," I have revised and updated the original English translation, then titled "Speech of General Bolívar to the Congress of Venezuela," which was both translated and published by the British merchant James Hamilton in Angostura within days of Bolívar's speech. It was republished in *Escritos del Libertador,* Vol.14. Rather than provide a new translation, I decided to keep as close to the spirit of Hamilton's original version, and to update its style (which follows Bolívar's original too closely, with its long sentences elaborately constructed with multiple clauses, and which causes confusion when rendered too literally into English). The text presented here retains most of Hamilton's phrasing, altered only for accessibility, readability and accuracy.

Document 11, the "Report on the Battle of Carabobo," is from the *Correo del Orinoco* 25 July 1821, with a few obvious errors corrected. The identity of the translator is unknown.

Documents 21, 22, 23 and 25 are my own original translations.

Documents 1, 4, 7, 8, 9, 12, 13, 14, 15 and 20 are translations by Frederick Fornoff, published in David Bushnell, ed., *El Libertador, Writings of Simón Bolívar* (Oxford: Oxford University Press, 2006). Fornoff succeeds in capturing the diversity of Bolívar's tone across a range of documents throughout the latter's career. We gratefully acknowledge the permission of OUP to use these texts.

In Documents 2, 3, 5, 16, 17, 18, 19 and 24, I have revised and updated Lewis Bertrand's translations published in Harold Bierck and Vicente Lecuna, eds., *Selected Writings of Bolívar* (New York: Colonial Press, 1951). While Bertrand's translations are generally accurate, they follow the Spanish original too literally on occasions, so I have tried to simplify phrasing and clarify meaning, often by reordering sentences. Often this has meant rewriting entire paragraphs. Documents 18 and 19 reproduce Bertrand's translation with no changes at all, as the flowery style suits the subject matter perfectly here.

Matthew Brown
Senior Lecturer in Latin American Studies
University of Bristol

Part I

FIGHTING FOR INDEPENDENCE

I

OATH TAKEN IN ROME

15 August 1805

Bolívar's second trip to Europe in 1804 transformed his life. During this time, he became sharply aware of the differences between Spain and its American colonies, and he resolved to dedicate his life to the struggle for independence. In May 1805 Bolívar was present in Milan to witness Napoleon Bonaparte crown himself Emperor. The next year in Rome, Bolívar formally committed himself before his friend and tutor Simón Rodríguez to dedicate his life to the independence of Spain's American colonies.

So then, this is the nation of Romulus and Numa, of the Gracchi and the Horaces, of Augustus and Nero, of Caesar and Brutus, of Tiberius and Trajan?[1] Here every manner of grandeur has had its type, all miseries their cradle. Octavian masks himself in the cloak of public piety to conceal his untrusting character and his bloody outbursts; Brutus thrusts his dagger into the heart of his patron so as to replace Caesar's tyranny with his own; Antony renounces his claim to glory to set sail on a whore's galleys with no reform projects, Sulla beheads his fellow countrymen, and Tiberius, dark as night and depraved as crime itself, divides his time between lust and slaughter. For every Cincinnatus there were a hundred Caracallas, a hundred Caligulas for every Trajan, a hundred Claudiuses for every Vespasian. This nation has examples for everything: severity for former times, austerity for republics, depravity for emperors, catacombs for Christians, courage for conquering the entire world, ambition for turning every nation on earth into a fertile field for tribute; women capable of driving the sacrilegious wheels of their carriages over the decapitated bodies of their parents; orators, like Cicero capable of stirring crowds to action; poets, like Virgil, for seducing with their song; satirists, like Juvenal and Lucretius; weak-minded philosophers, like Seneca; complete citizens, like Cato. This nation has examples for everything, except for the cause of humanity: corrupt Messalinas, gutless Agrippas, great historians, distinguished naturalists, heroic warriors, rapacious consuls, unrestrained sybarites, golden virtues, and foul crimes. But for the emancipation of the spirit, the elimination of cares, the exaltation of man, and the final perfectibility of reason, it has little or nothing. The civilization blowing in from the East has shown all its faces here, all its parts. But the resolution of the great problem of liberated man seems to have been something inconceivable, a mystery that would only be made clear in the New World.

I swear before you, I swear by the God of my fathers, I swear on their graves, I swear by my Country that I will not rest body or soul until I have broken the chains binding us to the will of Spanish might!

Simón Bolívar

NOTE

1 Bolívar climbed Monte Sacro in Rome in the company of his friend and tutor Simón Rodríguez on 15 August 1805. It is most likely that it was Rodríguez who later recalled this speech and wrote it down for posterity; it was first published in 1884. This may explain the amazingly literate references spouted by the young Bolívar (aged 22 at the time). The key phrases are the last three sentences, which express Bolívar's sense that this was a key turning point in his life—and they have not been doubted by historians. See Tomás Polanco Alcántara, *Simón Bolívar: Ensayo de una interpretación biográfica a través de sus documentos* (Caracas: Ediciones E.G., 1994), p.75, pp.101–5.

2

CARTAGENA MANIFESTO

15 December 1812

After the collapse of the First Venezuelan Republic in mid-1812 and the capture by Royalists of the Patriot leader Francisco de Miranda, Bolívar sought exile in the port of Cartagena de Indias, in nearby New Granada. In this manifesto, he sought to explain the reasons for the failure of independence in Caracas, blaming the ''principle of tolerance'' which had left Venezuela unguarded and unable to respond effectively to Spain's first attempts at reconquest.

In writing this memorial I want to spare New Granada from Venezuela's fate, and to release Venezuela from its present suffering. Please accept my words with indulgence, Fellow Citizens, and believe me that my intentions are laudable.

I am, Granadans, a son of unhappy Caracas, who escaped by a miracle from amidst her physical and political ruins. I have come here, ever faithful to the liberal and just system proclaimed by my country, to follow the banners of independence which wave so gloriously here.

Please allow me, inspired by patriotic zeal, to sketch briefly the reasons for Venezuela's destruction. I flatter myself that the terrible and exemplary lessons which that extinct Republic has supplied, may induce America to mend her ways and correct her obvious shortcomings in governance: those of unity, strength and energy.

The most grievous error committed by Venezuela in making her start on the political stage was, as none can deny, her fatal adoption of the system of tolerance—a system long condemned as weak and inadequate by every man of common sense, yet tenaciously maintained with an unparalleled blindness to the very end.

The first indication of senseless weakness demonstrated by our government was manifested in the case of the city of Coro, which, having refused to recognize the legitimacy of the government, was declared in rebellion and treated as an enemy. The supreme *junta*, instead of subjugating that undefended city, which would have surrendered as soon as our maritime forces had appeared off its harbor, gave it time to fortify itself and build up a strength so respectable that it later succeeded in subjugating the entire confederation almost as easily as we ourselves could previously have defeated it. The *junta* based its policy on poorly understood principles of humanity, which do not authorize governments to use force in order to liberate peoples who are ignorant of the value of their rights.

The codes consulted by our magistrates were not those which could teach them the practical science of government but were those devised by certain benevolent visionaries, who, creating fantastic republics in their imaginations, have sought to attain political perfection, assuming the perfectibility of the human race. Thus we were given philosophers for leaders, philanthropy for legislation, dialectic for tactics, and sophists for soldiers. Through such a distortion of principles, the social order was thoroughly shaken, and from that time on the State made giant strides toward its general dissolution, which, indeed, shortly came to pass.

Out of this crisis came a degree of impunity for crimes committed against the State. These crimes were committed without shame or fear, particularly by our born and implacable enemies, the European Spaniards, who had remained in our country solely to cause trouble, to keep it in continual turmoil and to foster as many conspiracies as our judges allowed them. These judges were too keen to pardon, even when the plots were of such magnitude as to endanger public welfare.

The doctrine which supported this procedure had its origin in the charitable maxims of a few writers who defend the thesis that no man is vested with the right to deprive another of his life even though he be guilty of the crime of treason. Under the cloak of this pious doctrine, every conspiracy was followed by a pardon; and every pardon by another conspiracy, which again brought pardon—all because liberal governments feel obliged to distinguish themselves through clemency. But this criminal clemency, more than anything else, contributed to the destruction of the structure whose construction we had still to complete!

This weakness was also behind the firm opposition to raising seasoned, disciplined troops, prepared to take their place on the field of battle and indoctrinated with the desire to defend liberty with success and honor. Instead, innumerable undisciplined militia units were formed. The exorbitant salaries paid to the officers of these units only exhausted the funds of the national treasury. Agriculture was destroyed because farmers were torn from their homes; this brought hatred upon the government which had forced them to abandon their families and take up arms.

"Republics," said our statesmen, "have no need for salaried soldiers to maintain their liberty. Every citizen will become a soldier when the enemy attacks us. Greece, Rome, Venice, Genoa, Switzerland, Holland and recently North America defeated their adversaries without the aid of mercenary troops, who stand always ready to support despotism and subjugate their fellow citizens."

With such political thinking and inaccurate reasoning, they deceived the simple-minded; but they did not convince the judicious who clearly understood the immense difference between the peoples, times, and customs of those republics and ours. It is true that they did not pay standing armies, but that was because these did not exist in antiquity; the safety and the honour of their states was entrusted to their civic virtues, their austere habits, and their military qualities—traits which we are very far from possessing. As regards the modern nations which have thrown off the yoke of tyranny, it is well known that they have maintained the number of hardened veterans necessary to insure their security. North America, however, being at peace with the world and protected by the sea, has not seen fit, in recent years, to maintain the complement of veteran troops needed to defend her borders and cities.

What followed in Venezuela was bitter evidence of the error of her calculations. The militia that went to meet the enemy, not knowing how to handle arms and unaccustomed to discipline and obedience, was routed at the very beginning of the last campaign, notwithstanding the heroic and extraordinary efforts of their leaders to lead them to victory. This defeat caused general discouragement among soldiers and officers, for it is a military truth that only battle-hardened armies are capable of surmounting the first reverses of a campaign. The novice soldier believes all is lost when he has once been routed. Experience has not proved to him that bravery, skill, and perseverance can mend misfortune.

The subdivision of the province of Caracas, which was planned, discussed and sanctioned by the Federal Congress, awakened and fomented bitter rivalry against the capital in the smaller cities and towns. "Which," said congressmen eager for control of their districts, "was the tyrant among cities and the leech of the state?" In this way the flame of civil war was kindled in Valencia, and was never extinguished even when its rebellion was defeated. It remained hidden under the surface and spread to the adjacent towns of Coro and Maracaibo.

These cities established communications with Valencia, thereby facilitating the entry of the Spaniards, which brought about the fall of Venezuela.

The dissipation of the public taxes for frivolous and harmful purposes, and particularly on salaries for an infinite number of office-holders, secretaries, judges, magistrates, and provincial and federal legislators dealt the Republic a mortal blow, since it was obliged to seek recourse in the dangerous expedient of issuing paper money, with no other guarantee than the probable revenues and backing of the Confederation. This new money, in the eyes of most people, was a direct violation of property rights, because they felt that they were being deprived of objects of intrinsic value in exchange for others of uncertain and even problematic worth. The paper money roused discontent among the otherwise indifferent people of the interior; hence, they called upon the commandant of the Spanish troops to come and free them from a currency which they regarded with more horror than slavery.

But what weakened the Venezuelan government most was the federal form it adopted in keeping with the exaggerated precepts of the rights of man. By authorizing each man to rule himself, the federal system disrupts social contracts and reduces nations to anarchy. This was what happened to the Confederation. Each province governed itself independently; and following this example, each city demanded like powers, based on the practice of the provinces and on the theory that all men and all peoples are entitled to establish whatever form of government they wish.

The federal system, although the most perfect and the most capable of providing for human happiness in society, is, nevertheless, the most contrary to the interests of our infant states. Generally speaking, our fellow-citizens are not yet able to exercise their rights themselves in the fullest measure, because they lack the political virtues that characterize true republicans—

virtues that are not acquired under absolute governments, where the rights and duties of the citizen are not recognized.

Moreover, what country in the world, however well trained and republican it may be, can, amidst internal factions and foreign war, be governed by so complicated and weak a system as the federal? No, this system cannot possibly be maintained during the turbulence of battles and political factions. It is essential that a government mold itself, so to speak, to the nature of the circumstances, the times, and the men that comprise it. If these are prosperity and peace, the government should be mild and protecting; but if they are turbulence and disaster, it should be stern and arm itself with a firmness that matches the dangers, without regard for laws or constitutions until happiness and peace have been reestablished.

Caracas was made to suffer severely by the shortcomings of the Confederation, which, far from aiding it, exhausted its treasury and war supplies. When danger threatened, the Confederation abandoned the city to its fate without assisting it with even a small contingent. The Confederation, moreover, created new difficulties, for the rivalry which developed between the federal and the provincial authorities enabled the enemies to penetrate deep into the heart of the State and to occupy a large part of the province before the question as to whether federal or provincial troops should go out to repel them was settled. This fatal debate resulted in a terrible and costly delay to our armies, for they were routed at San Carlos while awaiting the reinforcements needed for victory.

I believe that until we centralize our American governments, our enemies will gain irreversible advantages. We will inevitably fall into the horrors of civil warfare, and be miserably defeated by the handful of bandits who infest our lands.

The popular elections held by the simple people of the country and by the scheming inhabitants of the city added a further obstacle to our practice of federation, because the former are so ignorant that they cast their votes mechanically and the latter so ambitious that they convert everything into factions. As a result, Venezuela never witnessed a free and proper election and the government was placed in the hands of men who were either inept, immoral, or opposed to the cause of independence. Party spirit determined everything and, consequently, caused us more disorganization than the circumstances themselves. Our division, not Spanish arms, returned us to slavery.

The March 26 earthquake, it is true, was physically and morally destructive and can properly be termed the immediate cause of Venezuela's ruin. But the earthquake would not have produced such fatal results if at the time Caracas had been governed by a single authority. Acting promptly and vigorously, it could have repaired the damage without the hindrances and rivalries which delayed the recovery in the provinces, and left problems to fester until they became incurable.

If Caracas had established the simple government that its political and military situation required, instead of a slow-moving and insubstantial confederation, Venezuela would still exist and enjoy its freedom today!

Following the earthquake, the influence of the Catholic Church played a very considerable part in fomenting the insurgency of villages and smaller towns, and in bringing enemies into the country. They abused the sanctity of their ministry most sacrilegiously on behalf of the men who fomented civil war. Still, we must honestly admit that these traitorous priests were encouraged to commit the execrable crimes of which they are justly accused, because they knew that they enjoyed absolute immunity for their crimes, scandalously supported by Congress. This travesty of justice reached such a point that, following the insurrection of the city of Valencia, whose pacification cost nearly one thousand lives, not a single rebel was brought to justice. They all kept their lives, and many retained their property.

From the above it follows that among the causes that brought about Venezuela's downfall the nature of its Constitution ranks first, which, I repeat, was as contrary to Venezuela's interests as it was favourable to those of her adversaries; second, the spirit of misanthropy which possessed our governing officials; third, the opposition to the establishment of a military force which could save the Republic and repulse the Spanish attacks; fourth, the earthquake and its exploitation by fanaticism for its own advantage; and last, the internal factions which in reality were the fatal poison that laid the country in its tomb.

The South American peoples who aspire to freedom and independence will be able to learn some lessons from these tales of error and misfortune.

New Granada has seen Venezuela collapse and should therefore avoid the pitfalls that destroyed her. To this end, I submit, it is essential to reconquer Caracas in order to preserve New Granada's security. At first sight this project will appear far-fetched, costly, perhaps impracticable; but, examined closely, with foresight and careful reflection, it is as impossible to deny its necessity as to fail to put it into execution once it is proved advisable.

The first factor which offers itself in support of this operation is the fundamental cause of the destruction of Caracas, which was simply the contempt with which that city regarded the existence of an enemy who appeared of little account but who, taken in his true light, was not so at all.

Coro certainly could not have competed with Caracas, if physical preponderance had been the deciding factor. But in history the strongest peoples do not always win out. Often it is moral power that determines the political balance, and for this reason the government of Venezuela should surely have eradicated an apparently weak enemy which nevertheless enjoyed the support of the province of Maracaibo, by all those provinces which obeyed the Regency, by gold, as well as the cooperation of our eternal enemies, the Europeans who reside among us. Furthermore, Coro was supported by the clerical party, ever devoted to its master and companion, despotism. Coro had, above all, the unwavering support of every ignorant and superstitious person within the limits of our states. In the event, all it took was for one treacherous officer to summon the enemy in, and the entire political system was unbalanced, and all the unparalleled patriotic efforts of the defenders of Caracas were insufficient to prevent the fall of an edifice already tottering from the blow that it had received from one single man.

Applying the example of Venezuela to New Granada and putting it in the form of a ratio, we find that Coro is to Caracas as Caracas is to all America. This formula demonstrates the degree of danger which threatens this country. Given Spain's possession of the territory of Venezuela, she can easily draw upon it for men, provisions and munitions of war, and her armies, under the direction of leaders who have had experience against those great masters of warfare, the French, can move inland from the provinces of Barinas and Maracaibo to South America's deepest interior.

Spain today has a great number of daring and ambitious general officers, long accustomed to danger and to privations, who long to come here and seek an empire to replace that which they have just lost.

It is probable that as Spanish power collapses in the Iberian Peninsula there will be a tremendous emigration of men of all classes, particularly of cardinals, archbishops, bishops, canons and revolutionary clerics, all capable not only of subverting our incipient, faltering states, but of submerging the entire New World in frightful anarchy. The religious influence, the rule of civil and military domination, and all the prestige they can bring to bear upon the human spirit will be additional instruments which they will use in subjugating these countries.

Nothing will stand in the way of Spanish emigration. England will probably assist in the escape of a group whose departure would weaken Napoleon Bonaparte's forces in Spain, and would increase and add new life to England's own power in America. Neither France nor North America will be able to prevent this movement, and neither will we. All our efforts would be futile as none of us has a navy worthy of the name.

These fugitives will surely receive a warm welcome in the Venezuelan ports, as they will be coming to reinforce the oppressors of that country, and to undertake the conquest of the Independent States.

They will raise fifteen or twenty thousand men, whom their leaders, officers, sergeants, corporals, and veteran soldiers will rapidly drill and discipline. This army will be followed by another yet more terrible, of ministers, ambassadors, councilors, magistrates, all the ecclesiastical hierarchy and the grandees of Spain, whose trade is deceit and intrigue, and all bearing imposing titles designed to dazzle the multitude. And, descending like a torrent, they will overrun the land tearing Colombia's tree of liberty down to its very roots. The troops will fight on the field, but this army will battle us from their desks, using seduction and fanaticism for arms.

In order to guard against these calamities we will have no other recourse but to pacify our rebellious provinces as fast as we can, before turning our arms upon our enemies. In this way we will develop a body of soldiers and officers worthy to be called the nation's army.

Everything conspires to make us adopt this measure. In addition to the urgent necessity of closing the gates against the enemy, there are other reasons which force us to take the offensive, reasons so overwhelming that it would be a military error and a political blunder not to do so. We have been invaded, and consequently we are obliged to hurl the enemy back across the border. Moreover, it is a principle of the art of war that every defensive action is harmful and ruinous for those who wage it, as it weakens them without hope of recovery. Hostilities in enemy territory, however, are always advantageous by reason of the good that results from the enemy's misfortunes. Therefore on no account should we allow ourselves to go on the defensive.

We must also consider the present condition of the enemy, who is in a very critical position. The majority of his Creole soldiers have deserted at a time when he is obliged to garrison the patriot cities of Caracas, Puerto Cabello, La Guayra, Barcelona, Cumaná, and Margarita, where he keeps his stores. He does not dare to leave these towns unguarded for fear of a general insurrection the moment he departs. Thus it would not be impossible for our troops to reach the gates of Caracas without engaging in a single open battle.

As soon as we enter Venezuela we can be certain that we will be joined by thousands of brave patriots, who anxiously await our arrival in order to throw off the yoke of their tyrants and unite their efforts with ours in the defense of liberty.

The nature of the present campaign affords us the advantage of approaching Maracaibo by way of Santa Marta, and Barinas by way of Cúcuta.

Let us take advantage, therefore, of such a propitious moment. Reinforcements may arrive at any time from Spain, which would completely alter the state of affairs, and remove what might be a unique opportunity to assure the destiny of these states.

New Granada's honor absolutely demands that we teach these audacious invaders a lesson by pursuing them to their last strongholds. New Granada's glory depends upon its taking on the task of marching to Venezuela and liberating the cradle of Colombian independence, the martyrs and worthy people of Caracas. They address their cries only to their beloved New Granadan compatriots, and they await the arrival of these redeemers with despairing impatience. Let us march on to break the chains of the victims who groan in the dungeons, ever hopeful of rescue. Do not betray the trust they place in you. Do not be deaf to the cries of your brothers. Fly to avenge the dead, to give life to the dying, to bring freedom to the oppressed and liberty to all.

Simón Bolívar

3

DECREE OF WAR TO THE DEATH

15 June 1813

In early 1813 Bolívar returned to Venezuela from New Granada and found his armies fighting against Spanish forces who used all methods at their disposal. Bolívar felt this left him at a disadvantage. The War to the Death *proclamation, reproduced here, was Bolívar's response to the colonial authorities' repressive policies. Bolívar tried to make terms such as "republican" or "royalist" redundant by casting the conflict as a civil war between Spaniards and Americans. The exception he made for Venezuelans who had been fighting on the "wrong" side was crucial; it opened the possibility of forgiveness for Americans but denied it for Spaniards. Historians are divided as to the Decree's political impact; in practical terms it served to escalate the conflict's levels of violence even further and ushered in a period of severe bloodletting and massacres.*

Venezuelans!

An army of brothers, sent by the Supreme Congress of New Granada, has come to liberate you, and is now amongst you after having expelled the oppressors from the provinces of Mérida and Trujillo.

We have been sent to destroy the Spaniards, to protect Americans and to re-establish the republican governments which made up the Venezuelan Confederation. The states which we have liberated are once again ruled by their old constitutions and leaders, and they fully enjoy their liberty and independence. Our sole mission is to break the chains of servitude which still oppress some of our peoples. We have no intention of passing laws or exercising power, even though the laws of war might authorize us to do so.

We were so moved by your misfortune that we could not look on with indifference at the afflictions inflicted upon you by the Spanish barbarians, who have ravished you, plundered you and brought you death and destruction. They have violated the sacred rights of nations. They have broken the most solemn agreements and treaties. In sum, they have committed all possible crimes, reducing the Republic of Venezuela to the most terrible desolation. So it is that justice demands revenge, and necessity obliges us to take it. Let the monsters who infest Colombian soil, who have drenched it in blood, be cast out forever. Their punishment should be as great as their perfidy, so that we may wash away the stain of our ignominy. We must show all the world's nations that America's sons will not be offended with impunity.

Our resentment of the foul Spaniards is just, but our hearts are generous. We still leave open for them, one last time, the path of conciliation and friendship. We invite them once again to live amongst us in peace, on the condition that they renounce their crimes and in good faith join with us in working towards the destruction of the Spanish government of occupation, and the re-establishment of the Republic of Venezuela.

Every Spaniard who does not take up most active and efficient means to conspire with our just cause against tyranny, will be understood to be our enemy, and will be punished as a traitor to the country. They will then be put to death without appeal. In contrast, those Spaniards who join our ranks, with or without their weapons, and who lend their support to the good citizens who are struggling to throw off the yoke of tyranny, will be granted a general and absolute pardon. Military officers and civil leaders who come over to our side will retain their ranks and posts under the Venezuelan government. In a word, the Spaniards who render distinguished service to the state will be regarded and treated as Americans.

And you Americans, who out of error or perfidy have strayed from the path of justice, you should know that your brothers pardon you, and they sincerely lament your errors. We are convinced in our hearts that you can not be guilty and that only blindness or ignorance can have led you to commit crimes up to now. You should not fear the sword that comes to avenge you and to cut the ignominious ties with which your executioners have bound you to their own fate. You are hereby assured, with absolute impunity, of your honour, lives and property. The mere title of Americans will be your safeguard and your guarantee. We have brought our arms to protect you, and they will never be turned against a single one of our brothers.

This amnesty is extended even to the very traitors who most recently have committed acts of felony. It will be so religiously fulfilled that no possible reason, cause or pretext would oblige us to violate this promise, no matter how extraordinary and grievous the motives you may give to provoke our wrath.

Spaniards and Canarians,[1] even if you profess neutrality, know that you will die unless you work actively to bring about the liberation of America. Americans, know that you will live, even if you are guilty.

Simón Bolívar
Liberator of Venezuela, Brigadier of the Union, General in Chief of the Northern Army
Trujillo, 15 June 1813, 3rd Year of Independence

NOTE

1 The mention of "Spaniards and Canarians" indicates the intermediate identity of those born in the Canary Islands, who formed an

important immigrant group in Venezuela, particularly in the later colonial period. Bolívar labeled them as being more Spanish than American, however. See the relevant chapter in John Lynch, *Latin America between Colony and Nation: Selected Essays* (London: Palgrave and Institute of Latin American Studies, 2001).

4

MANIFESTO TO THE
NATIONS OF THE WORLD

20 September 1813

From his exile in Cartagena, Bolívar had been made a General in the army of the United Provinces of New Granada. He achieved some notable victories in the Andes as he positioned himself to lead his forces back into Venezuela, a series of victories known as the Admirable Campaign. In the middle of this expedition Bolívar penned the Manifesto to the Nations of the World, an early attempt to publicize the circumstances of the Venezuelan revolution, to justify his own conduct, and to blacken the reputations of the Spanish generals who had led the reconquest of Venezuela. This text is Bolívar's attempt to write the history of this reconquest and to inscribe within it his own motivation to fight for independence.

To the Nations of the World:

The people of these provinces, after having proclaimed their independence and freedom, were subjugated by an adventurer who—seizing power through usurpation and taking advantage of the consternation caused by an earthquake rendered frightening more through the ignorance and superstition of its victims than through the devastation it produced—invaded the territory, shedding American blood, robbing its inhabitants, and committing horrific atrocities that will appall and move you to sympathy once they have been sufficiently documented and presented for your consideration.

Meanwhile, for the purpose of avoiding calumny by our enemies, it is urgent and obligatory to provide you with a preliminary account, succinctly expressed since there is no other way of proceeding given the current situation to explain our present conduct, in the expectation that it will persuade you to condemn and abhor the conduct of our oppressors and to turn on them as enemies of the human species, authors of the most vicious crimes against justice and human rights, perpetrated shamelessly, and whose wickedness has yet to be punished by the nation in whose name they have shed our blood, savaged our citizens, and desolated our state.

Entering the province against the express orders of his superior, [Captain-General Fernando] Miyares, [Domingo de] Monteverde reached the outskirts of the city of Caracas, which had recently been destroyed by the terrible earthquake of 26 March 1812, subjugating a people confused and uncertain of his intentions. The only troops opposing him were unfortunately led by an officer who, motivated by ambition and violent passions, either failed to understand the risks or chose to sacrifice the freedom of his country to those personal motives, conducting himself arbitrarily and despotically to the extreme, upsetting not only his troops but also the personnel in the offices of public administration, and rendering the province or what was left of it null and void.

Monteverde, aided by several ignorant and corrupt clergymen who saw in our independence and freedom the destruction of their own empire, spared no resource in his effort to complete the seduction of the majority and to render the minority defenseless, the city destroyed, its population dispersed in the countryside, the people dying of hunger and misery, all of them terrorized by the assassinations carried out by [Eusebio] Antoñanzas, [José Tomás] Boves, and other subordinates whom he had stationed throughout the province, murdering ruthlessly, in cold blood and without due process, anyone considered a patriot, leaving the soldiers without direction or leaders, and the people uncertain as to their fate . . .

Such was the hapless condition of Caracas when the revolt of blacks, both slaves and freed, erupted in the eastern valleys and seacoast, incited, abetted, and sustained by the emissaries of Monteverde. This inhuman and savage mob, thirsty for blood and for the property of the patriots that had been mapped out and detailed in lists for them in Curiepe and Caucagua, marched against the population of Caracas, perpetrating in those valleys, and especially in the town of Guatire, the most horrific acts of murder, plunder, violence, and devastation. Those conquered—peaceful farmers, distinguished citizens, the innocent—were cut down with pistols and swords or were whipped barbarously after the armistice had been signed. Blood ran everywhere, and corpses were hung as ornaments in the streets and public squares of Guatire, Calabozo, San Juan de los Morros, and other towns inhabited by peaceful working people who, far from taking up arms, fled to the woods as the soldiers approached and who were rounded up, tied, and executed without any more formality, hearing, or trial than being forced to kneel down. Any officer or soldier was authorized to put to death anyone regarded as a patriot or whom they wanted to rob.

In this conflict Caracas—assaulted from the east by the blacks incited by the European Spaniards occupying the town of Guarenas, thirty miles from the city, and from the west by Monteverde, who was encouraged by his victory in Puerto Cabello, the only troops opposing him being those quartered in the town of La Victoria, weakened and demoralized by the arbitrary and violent actions of a hated leader—made an effort to surrender and in fact, after several attempts at negotiation, did sign articles of capitulation, by virtue of which her citizens surrendered their arms, supplies, and munitions to Monteverde, who marched unopposed into the city and took control.

The main article of capitulation, signed in San Mateo on 25 July 1812, stipulated that the lives and properties of the citizens would not be taken, that no one would be tried for political opinions expressed prior to the surrender, that no one would be harassed, and that there would be a general amnesty concerning past events. This treaty, entered into with a leader of the forces of a civilized European nation ever boastful of acting in good faith, eased the fears of even the most untrusting and timid, and everyone was resting from their recent exhaustion, not exactly content with the fate Providence had assigned them, but at least at peace and trusting in the guarantees offered in the armistice. They had fought enthusiastically to maintain their freedom, and even if they had failed in that effort, they took some consolation and satisfaction in having used all the means available to them.

On 29 July Monteverde entered Caracas at night and met with the Europeans and with distinguished groups and individuals, proffering to all of them the assurances which the surrender must have inspired, knowing full well that the perturbation, nervousness, and uncertainty manifested by the province were a consequence of desperation occasioned by acts of injustice and excess committed by the government of Spain and by the atrocious conduct of the officials Spain had assigned to administer and govern it. He must surely have known that people are never unhappy when treated fairly and governed equitably, and that the way to heal wounds is to follow the letter of the law. Violating these principles and the terms of the surrender, Monteverde set about arresting the most respected citizens, humiliating them publicly by placing them in stocks and, in order to mask his violation of law, spreading the word that those arrests and abuses were in retaliation for acts committed subsequent to the armistice. To make these charges seem credible, he issued a proclamation dated 3 August in which he swore that his promises were sacred, that his word was inviolable, and that these public proceedings were punishment for later infractions.

So the people, not daring to doubt this or even to conceive that Monteverde could be so hypocritical, malicious, and shameless, responded with uncertainty and timidity when, on 14 August, bands of Canary Islanders, Catalans, and other Europeans stationed throughout the city and countryside, issuing orders to subordinates in the interior of the province, began rounding up and arresting the Americans. The most decorated men from the period of the Republic were torn from the arms of their wives, children, and families in the dead of night; tied to the tails of the horses of shopkeepers, wine merchants, and other low brow people; dragged off ignominiously to jail, some shoved along on foot, others trussed hand and foot to a yoke for oxen, hauled off to the dungeons of La Guaira and Puerto Cabello; locked up there in arm and leg irons; and subjected to the inhuman vigilance of savage men, some of whom had been themselves persecuted during the time of the revolution; and worst of all, this was all done under the pretext that these wretched captives were the instigators of a revolutionary conspiracy against the terms of the surrender. In this way uncertainty was perpetuated, and everyone held back, until the slanderous felony was accepted as fact; then they fled into the woods to seek safety among the wild animals, leaving the cities and towns deserted, so that the only people to be seen in their streets and public roads were the Europeans and Canary Islanders armed with pistols, swords, and blunderbusses, menacing everyone and spewing forth acts of revenge, perpetrating atrocities against women as well as men, and committing the most shameless acts of plunder, so that there was not a single one of Monteverde's officers not wearing a shirt, or a cassock, or the trousers of some American whom he had stripped. Even some officers who served as garrison commanders participated in such abuse, as for instance in the public square of La Guaira, where the atrocious [Francisco Javier] Cervériz burst into the dungeons of that port to heap insults on the very victims in whose garments he was dressed from head to foot.

These men took possession of everything. They camped in the *haciendas* and homes of the villagers, and they destroyed or rendered useless whatever they couldn't take. Given the brevity demanded by the circumstances, it is impossible to depict the condition of that province. The most honourable men, heads of families, fourteen-year-old boys, priests who modeled their lives on the Gospels and true maxims of Jesus Christ, eighty-year-old men, innumerable men who had no part, who could not have had a part in the revolution, were locked in dark, hot, humid dungeons, burdened with chains and leg irons, utterly miserable. Some suffocated right there in their cells. Others could not endure the grief and martyrdom and gave up their lives without medical or spiritual aid, which were ruthlessly denied them, or provided only when the dying man was too weak to move or speak. In the streets the only sounds were the cries of unhappy women calling to their husbands, mothers crying for their sons, brothers for their brothers, relatives for relatives. The house of the tyrant echoed with the howls and weeping of countless wretched women, and he took pleasure in this homage which grew in proportion to the smoke rising from the victims, while his subordinates, especially his countrymen from the Canaries, far from being moved to pity, insulted the women with barbarous expressions and leers whereby they demonstrated how much pleasure they derived from the humiliation of the people of that land.

Amid the confusion of the widespread imprisonment, only five or six persons managed to secure passports from Monteverde allowing them to leave the province. In his stupidity the tyrant, whose decrees were purely arbitrary or issued to please some favourite, made the mistake of issuing me one. Passport in hand

and wasting no time, I accompanied my compatriots to the island of Curacao and from there to Cartagena where, relating what was happening in Caracas, I aroused the just indignation of that generous people. Its leaders took upon themselves the grievances of the Caracans, supported our claims before the Congress of New Granada and in the city of Santa Fe, and then we were witness to the concern Americans take for other Americans. The public response of the Granadans was unanimous in its expression of righteous indignation toward our oppressors, and the representatives of the provinces communicated their outrage to their delegates, urging them to furnish every possible aid to their oppressed brothers. The general enthusiasm matched the fire that burned inside me to liberate my country, and by virtue of my urging and my praiseworthy and holy fervour I found myself in command of a contingent of troops small in number but inspired by the virtuous desire to liberate their brothers from the unbearable yoke of tyranny, injustice, and violence. I entered the province, defeating the tyrant's armies wherever they showed their faces. They could not stand up against the might of free men, generous, brave, and determined, who had vowed to exterminate the enemies of the freedom to which the people of America so rightfully aspire. This enthusiasm grew and was kindled to even greater intensity by the discovery, upon our entry into the province, of the horrible ravages caused by the Spaniards and Canarians. Then we saw with our own eyes the devastation of the *haciendas*, the destruction of property, the atrocities against some and the murder of others. We wept over the ruins, and joining our tears to those of so many widows and orphans standing beside the remains of their husbands, fathers, and brothers, whose bodies were still tied to the posts where they were shot or scattered about the fields, we repeated our vow to liberate our brothers from the cells, dungeons, and jails where they lay as if buried, and from the cruel, infamous yoke of such fiendish oppressors.

Until that moment, our state of mind and our conduct in the waging of war had been concordant with the practice of civilized nations, until we discovered that the enemy routinely took the lives of prisoners whose only crime was the defense of liberty, falsely branding them as insurgents, as happened to those executed by Don Antonio Tízcar, commander of Monteverde's troops in Barinas, the prisoners being found guilty by a jury composed of judges without jurisdiction and in violation of the most basic formalities demanded by nature and by the universal code of law, civilized or not, the sentence being ordered and then carried out by a person lacking all legal authority. We resolved to wage a war to the death, sparing only the Americans, for otherwise our enemies' advantage was insuperable, they being in the habit of killing our prisoners under the pretext that they were rebels, while we treated ours with the decency proper to our character and with every consideration demanded by humanity.

The results have validated and demonstrated the justice and necessity of our conduct, because once the Spaniards and Canarians were deprived of the advantage with which they had previously fought and now realized that their lot was equal to ours, they ceased to regard themselves as our masters and began to fear us as men. Then it became palpably clear what great cowards evil men are and how unwarranted our fear of tyrants is; all one need do is stand up to despots to send them running shamelessly away. We have seen how these brave men, who earlier behaved like wild beasts as they assaulted defenseless citizens, running them through and hacking them to pieces with their swords, turned and fled from a handful of our soldiers who charged their ranks, though they greatly outnumbered us. Between Cúcuta and Caracas they only showed their faces seven times, each time being routed immediately, and their terror was so great that the famous Monteverde, who had formerly swaggered around Caracas in imitation of the despots of Asia in manner, style and conduct, abandoned Valencia, leaving behind an enormous battery of artillery, to take hasty refuge in Puerto Cabello, with no recourse but to surrender. Even so, as we approached Caracas several emissaries from the governor came to us, offering to surrender, and although they were utterly defenseless and had no means to oppose us, we granted them their lives and property and a total amnesty. But you should know that this mission was a scheme to gain time so they could embark at La Guaira, taking their weapons and ammunition with them and jamming the artillery. These scoundrels left with as many men as they could prior to the formal surrender, leaving the Spaniards and Canarians to face our just wrath.

It is not possible to convey the pusillanimity of the coward [Manuel del] Fierro, or the state of chaos and anarchy in which he left the city of Caracas when he so shamelessly escaped. That we did not encounter a bloodbath on our entry into the capital is evidence of an enormous generosity of spirit, a quality ever manifest among the Americans. We did discover shops and stores broken into and looted by the very people who had previously been robbed by Monteverde and his henchmen, but even though the Europeans and Canarians were at the mercy of an angry population, they were treated with moderation. The wives of the Spaniards and many of their husbands who were trying to escape carrying their possessions in bundles were treated with respect in their misfortune. Their flight toward the nearby port was so disorderly and confused that many dropped their weapons, others threw off their clothing in order to run faster, believing the enemy was pursuing them, and others finally abandoned themselves to their fate cursing the cowardly and inhuman leader who had put them in this situation. Such was the picture of Caracas I saw as I approached the capital.

This is not the time to present to the world a manifesto detailing the excesses of our enemies or describing our military operations. Those will emerge from the trial that must be held and for which the necessary instructions are being issued, based on the report I have given and will convey to the honourable Congress of New Granada for her own glory and the satisfaction of America. As stated at the beginning, our intention is merely to resist slander and convey succinctly the justice of our complaints against Spain. The *Cortes* and the Regency of Cádiz not only viewed with unconcern Monteverde's insubordination to his general, Miyares, but they applauded his usurpation of the latter's authority, promoting him to Captain-General of Caracas. Not only did they look with indifference on the scandalous violation of the surrender at San Mateo, on the arrests and maltreatment of the citizens, the destruction of their jobs, the acts of plunder, the assassinations, and the atrocities which Monteverde, his officers and soldiers committed and have continued to commit since they took refuge in Puerto Cabello, but even today the newspapers and journals report that the question of whether the surrender ought or ought not to be honored is still being argued in the *Cortes*. Eight of the men involved in the violation remain free on the Peninsula, and in the interim Monteverde has continued to act capriciously and willfully, without restraint or fear of disciplinary action.

But there is one further fact that proves better than any other the criminality and complicity of the government of Cádiz. The *Cortes* established the constitution of the kingdom, which is clearly a product of the enlightenment, knowledge, and experience of its members. Monteverde regarded this constitution as something irrelevant, or as something opposed to his ideas and those of his advisors. Finally he decides to publish it in Caracas. He does so, and for what purpose? Not only to mock it but to insult it and contradict it by deeds wholly contrary to it. He invites everyone to assemble, urging calm and suggesting that the ark of peace is at hand; the naïve citizens assemble, many of them crawling out of the caves in which they were hiding; they believe he is speaking in good faith. His intent was to entrap those who had escaped, so he publishes a copy of the Spanish constitution, a document based on the holy principles of freedom, property, and security, while simultaneously sending out bands of Spaniards and Canarians to arrest and carry off ignominiously those unwary enough to have assembled to witness and celebrate its publication.

This is a truth as notorious as all of those that have been described in this paper, and it will be further explained in the manifesto being drawn up. In the province of Caracas, the Spanish constitution has no validity; the Spaniards themselves mock it, insult it. Following its publication they make arrests without justification, shackle prisoners with chains and handcuffs at the whim of the commanders and judges; and put prisoners to death without legal formalities or trials, as Tízcar did in Barinas in May of this year, as [Antonio] Zuazola did in Aragua, and Boves in Espino, sending off groups of prisoners indiscriminately to jails, dungeons, and prisons, while the territorial *Audiencia*, following Monteverde's advice, establishes a procedure and a conduct diametrically opposed to the spirit and letter of the constitution. In view of all this, and the indifference or tacit consent of the Spanish government, can America hope to improve its lot as a dependent of that peninsula? Can America be considered criminal and insurgent in its efforts to recover its freedom? And with regard to Caracas, can anyone call into question the resolve and conduct of General Simón Bolívar and his compatriots and fellow soldiers for trying to rescue brothers, friends, and relatives from the cells, jails, dungeons, and pens where they lay oppressed, humiliated, and abused? Here we put aside the principles on which Venezuela proclaimed her freedom and independence, observing instead the long list of reasons we had for undertaking to break the yoke of her oppressors, justifying our conduct by a minimal and approximate sketch of the insults, atrocities, and crimes of Monteverde and his accomplices, especially his fellow Canarians. Those can be reduced to a few articles: the scandalous infraction of the surrender at San Mateo; the murders perpetrated throughout the province, the killing of prisoners of war, people who had surrendered, who were unarmed, simple farmers, peaceful citizens, and even people already imprisoned; the inhuman, ignominious, cruel, and brutal treatment of distinguished, decorated citizens; the occupation of *haciendas* and other properties; acts of plunder tolerated and authorized; the senseless, unwarranted destruction of places of employment where Americans worked; the suffering of so many devastated families; the homelessness, sadness, and weeping of the most respected women in the towns, who wandered through the streets exposed to lewd insolence and the savage behaviour of the Canarians, city thugs, sailors, and soldiers.

This then, Nations of the World, is the most succinct idea I can give you at this time of my conduct in the project which I conceived to liberate Caracas from the tyrant Monteverde, under the auspices of the virtuous, humane, and generous people of New Granada. I stand before you with my weapons still at the ready, and I will not put them down until I eradicate every last Spaniard from the provinces of Venezuela that have most recently experienced the excess of their tyranny, their injustice, their perfidy, and their atrocities. I will fill with glory the campaign I have undertaken for the health of my country and the happiness of my fellow citizens, or I will die in the effort, demonstrating to the entire world that the Americans are not to be scorned or slandered with impunity.

Nations of the World: Venezuela owes you the consideration of not letting you concern yourselves with the false and misleading accounts which those scoundrels will contrive to discredit our conduct. In short order, the precise and documented manifesto of everything that happened in the year 1812 and up to the present time in these provinces will be published. Suspend your judgment for the moment, and if you wish to seek out the truth on your own, Caracas not only welcomes you but eagerly awaits the arrival in its ports of all able men who come seeking refuge among us and who can help us with their skill and knowledge, without concern for their place of origin.

Simón Bolívar
Brigadier General of the Union, and Commander-in-Chief of the Army of the North, Liberator of Venezuela, etc.
General Headquarters of Valencia, 20 September 1813

5

MANIFESTO OF CARÚPANO

7 September 1814

The Spanish reconquest of the Venezuelan Second Republic was completed by José Tomás Boves and Francisco Morales, whose decisive command of llanero troops exposed and exploited the frailties of the converted militias and volunteers commanded by Bolívar. On the eve of sailing once more into exile, Bolívar issued this document, the Manifesto of Carúpano, which accepted that he had been culpable in Venezuela's failure and expressed a forlorn sense of helplessness. Even then, however, at one of the lowest points of his military career, Bolívar exuded faith in the process of revolution, that he would have his revenge and emerge, ultimately, triumphant.

Citizens,

Unhappy is the leader who, responsible for the calamities or crimes of his country, is obliged to defend himself before a tribunal of the people against the charges which his fellow citizens make against his conduct. But happy indeed is the leader who, amidst the pitfalls of war, politics and public misfortunes, preserves his honor intact, and, innocent, comes forward to exact of his companions in misery a just decision respecting his innocence.

I have been chosen by the fortunes of war to break your chains, and I have also been, let us say, the instrument that Providence has used to fill your measure of afflictions to the brim. Yes, I have brought you peace and freedom, but in the wake of these inestimable benefits war and slavery have accompanied me. Victory guided by justice has always been our aim even to the very ruin of the fair capital of Caracas, which we wrested from the hands of her oppressors. New Granada's warriors retained their laurels as they fought Venezuela's conquerors. Caracas's soldiers were also crowned with good fortune against the fierce Spaniards who wished to subject us once more. If an inconsistent destiny has caused victory to alternate between us and our enemies, it has only been because some unexplainable madness has come over American peoples, forcing them to take up arms to destroy their liberators, and to restore the scepter to their tyrants. Thus it appears that Providence, to our humiliation and glory, has determined that our brothers shall be our conquerors and that only our brothers shall triumph over us. The liberating army has exterminated the enemy bands, but it could not, nor should it, exterminate the people for whose good it has waged hundreds of battles. It is not right to destroy men who do not wish to be free, nor is freedom that which prevails under the sway of arms and over the opinion of fanatics whose depravity of mind induces them to love chains as the bonds of society.

Deplore, then, only those compatriots who, prompted by the fury of discord, have submerged you in this sea of calamities, the mere sight of which makes Nature tremble, and which is so horrible that it is impossible to describe. Your brothers, and not the Spaniards, have plunged the knife into your breast, spilled your blood, burned your homes, and condemned you to exile. Let your outcries be directed against those blind slaves who would fetter you with the chains that they themselves bear. Harbour no malice toward the martyrs, who, as fervent defenders of your liberty, have recklessly shed their blood on every field and faced every danger to save you from death or ignominy. Be just in your agony even as the cause producing it is just. Do not be so moved by your sufferings, my Citizens, as to regard your protectors and friends as accomplices in imaginary crimes of either intention or omission. Those who direct your destinies, no less than their supporters, have had no other purpose than to obtain for you a perpetual happiness, which for them should mean immortal glory. But if events did not turn out as they had intended, and if unparalleled disasters have frustrated their laudable enterprise, this has not been due to their ineptitude or cowardice. No, it was the inevitable consequence of a gigantic project, beyond all human forces. The destruction of a government whose origins are lost in the obscurity of time, the overthrow of established principles; the changing of customs, the refinement of public opinion; and in fact, the establishment of liberty in a country of slaves is a work impossible to execute rapidly. It is indeed so far beyond any human power that our excuse for having failed to achieve what we desire is inherent in the cause which we pursue, for even as Justice warrants the boldness of undertaking it, the impossibility of its accomplishment only reflects the inadequacy of the means available. It is commendable, noble and sublime to seek to vindicate Nature violated by tyranny. Nothing can compare with the glory and grandeur of this project, and even if desolation and death should be our reward, there would still be no reason to condemn it. Justice compels us to act even though our goals are not close at hand.

In vain have innumerable victories been won through unprecedented efforts and the bitter loss of our heroic soldiers' blood. The edifice of our glory has been brought down by only a few of our enemies' victories. The majority of the people have been led astray by religious fanaticism and seduced by the enticements of a devouring anarchy. To the torch of liberty, which we have offered to America as the guide and the object of our efforts, our enemies have applied the incendiary brand of discord, of devastation, and the strong enticement of usurped honours and fortunes for men who have been debased by the yoke of servitude and reduced to brutishness by the doctrine of superstition. How, with no other support than Truth and Nature, could the mere theory of a political philosophy prevail against Vice which, armed with an unbridled license and having no restraints other than its own capacity, has been transformed overnight through the prestige of religion into political virtue and Christian charity? No! Ordinary men are not able to appreciate the eminent worth of the reign of liberty when they are offered blind ambition and base greed instead. Our fate has depended upon the decision of this important question. This choice of liberty over ambition lay in the hands of our compatriots who, deluded, decided against us. All else that followed flowed from a determination more dishonourable than fatal, and more to be regretted in its essence than in its results.

It is malicious and stupid to blame public men for the events that occur naturally within a state. In times of turbulence, shock and disagreement, a general or leader does not have the power to check the torrent of human passions which, agitated by the forces of revolutions, grow in proportion to the force which resists them. Even when the leaders' grave errors or their violent passions do cause injury to the Republic, the harm must be objectively measured and its causes sought in the original sources of all misfortune: human frailty and the power of chance to influence events. Man is the feeble pawn of fortune, which he often tries to understand through reason, though never with certainty, because our realm is so far from the higher sphere of things. To expect politics and war to proceed in keeping with our plans, while we labour in doubt aided only by the force of our intentions and limited support which is at best arbitrary, is like seeking to achieve, through human resources, results attainable only by a divine power.

Far from entertaining the insane presumption of considering myself blameless for my country's catastrophe, I suffer on the country the deepest grief, for I regard myself as the accursed instrument of its frightful miseries. Yet I am innocent, because my conscience has never been party to any willful error or act of malice, even though it may, of course, have advised me wrongly and negatively. My heart encourages me to be convinced of my innocence. The testimony before you is authentic, though it may appear that the delirium of pride is speaking. This is why I have not replied to any of the accusations made against me in good or bad faith. I reserve this act of justice, which I demand for my own vindication, for a tribunal of wise men who should judge my conduct during my mission to Venezuela, with understanding and righteousness. I refer to the Supreme Congress of New Granada, to that august body which sent me with its armies to your assistance. These armies served heroically on the field of honour until the very last man had fallen.

It is just and necessary that my public life be examined carefully and judged impartially. It is just and necessary that I give satisfaction to any whom I may have offended and that I be cleared of the erroneous charges which I have not deserved. This major judgment must be pronounced by the sovereign power that I have served. I assure you that it will be the most solemn judgment possible and that my actions will be supported by irrefutable documents. Then you will know whether I have been unworthy of your trust or have earned the name of Liberator. I swear to you, beloved Compatriots, that this august title which your gratitude bestowed upon me when I came to strike off your chains will not be without purpose. I swear to you that as Liberator, living or dead, I will always be worthy of the honour you have accorded me; nor is there any human power on earth which can stay the course which I have set for myself—to return a second time, by that western road already drenched with so much blood and adorned with so many laurels, to make you free. Have hope, Compatriots! The noble, the good Granadan people will return, eager to earn new trophies, to give you new support, and once more to bring you freedom, unless you previously achieve it by your own valour.

Indeed, Compatriots, your own virtues can wage war successfully against the frenzied multitude which can not perceive its own interests or honour. Freedom has never been subjugated by tyranny. Do not compare your physical forces with the enemies', because spirit and matter cannot be compared. You are men, they are beasts. You are free, they are slaves. Fight, and you will win. God grants victory to those who persevere.

Simón Bolívar
Carúpano, 7 September 1814

6

THE JAMAICA LETTER

6 September 1815

In exile in Jamaica Bolívar sought to attract international support for his planned return to Venezuela, which he envisaged as part of a larger continental plan for liberation of Spain's colonies. Like his predecessor Francisco de Miranda, Bolívar recognized that he needed to win Britain's support, or at the very least persuade Britain not to intervene on Spain's side in the independence wars. This letter, written in exile in a British colony to a British merchant, contains some of Bolívar's most succinct analyses of the obstacles faced by nation-builders in the Americas and his proposals as to how they could be negotiated and overcome for future glory. The letter's aims were ultimately achieved: Britain declared itself neutral in the conflict between Spain and its colonies whilst turning a blind eye to the recruitment of mercenaries to fight under Bolívar, and to the efforts of British businessmen to supply the Venezuelans with uniforms, arms and credit.

I have now the honour of replying to your letter, forwarded to me through our mutual friend Mr.——, which I received with the greatest satisfaction. I feel most gratefully impressed by the lively interest you have been kind enough to take in the cause of my country, evidenced by the concern you express for the misfortunes with which she has been oppressed by the Spaniards from the period of her discovery even to the present day.[1] I am also anxious to respond to your request for information relative to the history of my nation. But the want of necessary documents and books, added to the slender knowledge I possess of such an immense, varied, and unknown country as the great South American continent, render it, in my opinion, impossible to answer your questions. Even Baron Humboldt himself, with his versatility of talent, could scarcely reply to them with much accuracy. Although some of the statistics and some of the revolutionary events are known, I can confidently tell you that the most important events are obscured, as it were, in darkness, and consequently none but the most vague and imperfect conjectures can be formed of them. It would be idle to fix what may be the future fate and real intentions of the Americans, whose nation, because of its physical possessions, the vicissitudes of war, and the line of its own and European policies, is subject to the same uncertainties as all other nations in history.

I am writing this letter because I consider myself bound to give every attention to your much esteemed favour, on account of your very kind and philanthropic views. I am afraid that you will not find the brilliant explanations you hope for, rather only a simple presentation of my thoughts and wishes.

"Three ages are elapsed," you observe, "since the commencement of those barbarities which were committed by the Spaniards in the great hemisphere of Colombia." Contemporaries had refused to believe in these barbarous stories, seeing them as fables instead which fell so far below the depravity of human nature that they could not be credited. Yet they are confirmed by texts which establish their unhappy truths. The philanthropic bishop of Chiapas, Apostle of the Indies, [Bartolomé de Las Casas] has left posterity a brief narrative, extracted from the legal documents found in Sevilla. The barbarism of the conquest as recounted by Las Casas is acknowledged by all people of consideration and eminence, and even by the tyrants' own secret documents. Archbishop

Dávila Padilla, Philip II's chronicler, tells us that the celebrated Spanish writers Herrera, Muñoz, Torquemada, and others, all copied and venerated his faithful text.[2] In a word, all impartial people have acknowledged the zeal, truth, and virtue displayed by Las Casas, that friend to humanity, who fearlessly and boldly denounced the most horrid crimes committed under the influence of a sanguinary frenzy, before his own government and his contemporaries. I shall say nothing to you of the English, French, Italians and Germans who have written about America, as you are without doubt sufficiently acquainted with them.

I felt deep gratitude when I read the paragraph in your letter wherein you express a hope, "that the same success which then attended the Spanish arms may now follow those of her opponents, the oppressed children of America." I take this worthy hope as a prediction. If justice be allowed to determine the contests of men, then success will crown our efforts. Doubt it not: The destiny of America is irrevocably fixed. The different portions of that immense monarchy were only linked together by an illusory tie. What *then* united them, *now* divides them. Our hatred for the Peninsula is vaster than the ocean which separates her from us. It would be easier to join the two continents than to conciliate the two countries. Before, we were tied to Spain by the habits of obedience to constituted authorities, an interchange of interests, knowledge, and religion, a reciprocal benevolence, and a tender concern for the mother country and the glory of our ancestors. In sum, all our hopes, all our wishes, lay centered in Spain. From them came a principle of submission which appeared eternal, although the misconduct of our governors gradually weakened this feeling of attachment to the principles of government. Today, the opposite is true: we are threatened by death and the most terrible dishonour by a disgraced wicked stepmother![3] But the veil has at last been cast off. Although she wished to keep us in darkness, we have seen light. We have been free, but our enemies want to enslave us once more. We are fighting defiantly for our liberty, and desperation seldom fails to bring victory in its wake.

We should not lose faith in our destiny just because our successes have been partial and incomplete thus far. Our Liberators are victorious in some areas, whilst in others, our enemies have their advantage. But what is the result? Is not the contest undecided? Do we not see the whole of this new world in motion, armed in our defense? Let us cast our eyes around, and we shall see, throughout the whole extent of this immense hemisphere, a simultaneous struggle.

The warlike disposition of the River Plate provinces has cleared that territory, and continued in victory to Peru and Cuzco, disturbed Arequipa, and alarmed the royalists of Lima. Nearly a million inhabitants enjoy their liberty there.

The territory of Chile, populated by 800,000 souls, is resisting subjugation by its enemy. The Royalists will fail there because those who long ago put an end to the conquests of this enemy, the free and indomitable Araucanians, are the neighbors and compatriots of those who seek Independence. The sublime example of the Araucanians is proof to those fighting in Chile that a people who love independence will eventually achieve it.[4] The Viceroyalty of Peru, with over one and a half million inhabitants, is without doubt the most submissive, as there the greatest sacrifices have been extorted from them for the royal cause. Yet although there are various reports regarding that beautiful portion of America, it is known to be very far from a state of tranquility, and it will not be able to resist the overwhelming torrent which threatens most of the Peruvian provinces.

New Granada, which may be considered the heart of South America, obeys its general Independent government. The only exceptions are the kingdom of Quito, which struggles to restrain its enemies from a warm partiality to the cause of their country, and the provinces of Panama and Santa Marta which still suffer Spanish oppression.[5]

With respect to heroic but unhappy Venezuela, her disasters have been so numerous, and have occurred with such rapidity, that she is now almost reduced to a state of absolute want and dejected misery, and this was one of those fine provinces which constituted the pride of America. Venezuela was said to contain nearly a million inhabitants, and it can with truth be asserted that a quarter of them have been sacrificed by the sword, by earthquakes, by hunger, by pestilence, by fatigue from displacement. All these, with the exception of earthquakes, were the results of warfare.

According to Baron Humboldt, in 1808 there were some 7,800,000 souls in New Spain, including Guatemala. Since then, however, the insurrection which has agitated virtually all her provinces has seriously reduced Humboldt's exact calculation. Recent publications faithfully describe the sanguinary crimes committed in that opulent empire, where more than a million men have perished.[6]

The islands of Puerto Rico and Cuba, which jointly have a population of seven or eight hundred thousand souls, are the places where Spaniards retain possession with the smallest difficulty, as they are not within the immediate influence of the Independents. But are they not Americans? Are they not wronged? Will they not desire their emancipation?

This broad description presents a military conflict measuring two thousand leagues in length, and nine hundred in breadth, in which sixteen million human beings are either defending their rights, or bowing under the oppressions of the Spanish government. Spain formerly possessed the most extensive empire in the universe, but is now not only too impotent to rule the new world, but insufficient to maintain itself in the old! And will civilized Europe, commercial Europe which values liberty so much, will Europe allow Spain to desolate the most beautiful portion of the globe?

What madness it is for our enemy to suppose that we are to be reconquered by a nation without a navy, without money and without soldiers! As for her army, it is barely sufficient to keep her own subjects in obedience, and wholly inadequate to defend her from her neighbours. Besides, can a nation like Spain, which lacks manufacturing, productive land, arts, sciences, and even policy, can Spain really monopolize the trade of half the world? Even supposing the success of this rash undertaking, even supposing she could bring about reconciliation, would not our heirs within twenty years come to return to the grand and patriotic designs which we are now fighting for, even though they had been temporarily united with the reconquering Europeans?

I am decidedly of the opinion that Europe would confer a great benefit on Spain, were she to dissuade her from her obstinate temerity, as it would at least spare her the expenditure of her revenue, and prevent the effusion of blood. Then might she direct her attention to more laudable and proper pursuits, and might ground her prosperity and power on more durable foundations than those of uncertain conquests, precarious commerce, and violent exactions from people who are distant, unfriendly, and powerful. Europe herself, on a principle of wisdom and policy, should have prepared and carried into effect the grand project of American Independence, not merely because "the balance of power" requires it, but because it would have been the most legal and certain method of obtaining overseas trade herself. It falls to Europe, by every principle of equity, to explain Spain's true interests, as it is not agitated by the contending emotions which exist in Spain.

"The criminal way," as you say, "in which Bonaparte captured Charles IV and Ferdinand VII, kings of the nation which three centuries ago treacherously imprisoned two American monarchs, is a conclusive instance of divine retribution," and at the same time a proof that, as Heaven sustains the just cause of the colonists, God will grant us our independence.

It seems that you allude to Montezuma, king of Mexico, who was taken prisoner by [Hernán] Cortés, and killed, according to Herrera, by him (though Solis says he was killed by the people). You also allude to Atahualpa, Inca of Peru, who was destroyed by Francisco Pizarro and Diego Almagro. However, there is so great a difference between the fate of the Spanish kings and those of America, that they cannot be compared. The former were treated with dignity, allowed to live, and at length restored to their liberty, and Ferdinand to the throne. The latter suffered unheard-of torments, and were treated most disgracefully and contemptuously. Though Cuauhtemoc, Montezuma's successor, was indeed honoured as a prince, and the crown was placed on his head, it was as a mark of derision, not of respect, reminding him of his fall before torturing him. The fate of Catzontzin, the king of Michoacán, the Zipa of Bogotá and all the indigenous nobles and dignitaries who opposed Spanish power of Spain, was similar to that of this unhappy monarch!

But, in returning from this digression to your letter, I observe you remark that you have

> for some months past, made many reflections as to the situation of the Americans, and their future hopes. I take a great interest in their success, but have not much information as to their actual condition, or that to which they aspire. I am infinitely desirous of knowing the population of every province, as well as its policy. Whether they wish for republics or monarchies, or whether one great republic, or one great monarchy. All information of this nature which you can afford me, or point out the sources from which I may derive such knowledge, I shall esteem as a most particular favour.

The great interest you take in the fate of my country entitles you to my warmest gratitude. Sir, please accept my desire to meet your wishes, as a tribute of my sincere esteem. I have already stated the population, as well as it can be ascertained from the data with which we are furnished, but which for a thousand reasons cannot be exact. Most of the inhabitants live in rural areas, and many do not have permanent residences, as they are labourers or shepherds, scattered throughout spacious and immense woods and plains, surrounded by beautiful and extensive lakes and rivers. Who could form a complete statement of the numbers in such territories?

In addition, forced indigenous tribute, the sufferings of the slaves, the taxes, tithes and duties which press on the laborers, all drive poor Americans from their homes. And this is without mentioning the war, which has already exterminated one eighth of the population, and dispersed the greater part of the remainder. When this is considered, the difficulty of arriving at any correct statement of population and resources will be found insurmountable.

It is still more difficult to divine what the new world's fate will be, to establish any principles with respect to its politics, or to predict what nature or kind of government it will ultimately adopt. All statements relative to the future condition of this country appear to me hazardous and rash. Could it have been foreseen, during the early periods of human existence, when mankind was obscured in uncertainty, ignorance, and error, what regime would be adopted for their preservation? Who would have ventured to say whether one nation would be a republic, and another a monarchy? Who would have predicted which would be small, and which would be great? This is where we find ourselves. We are, as it were, a race by ourselves; we possess a world apart, surrounded by different seas; we are as yet strangers to almost all the arts and sciences, although we are, to a degree, experienced in the common usages of civil society.

I consider the present state of America as similar to that of imperial Rome when it was decaying. Every part formed its own political system, agreeable to its interests and situation, or followed the particular ambition of certain chiefs, families, or corporations. There is one remarkable difference, which is that in Europe the dispersed tribes reestablished their ancient customs, with such alterations as were required by circumstances. But we hardly preserve a vestige of what we were, being neither Indians nor Europeans, but rather a race somewhere between the original natives and the European Spaniards. We are Americans by birth and our rights are those of Europe, so we have to dispute and fight for these contending interests, and to persevere in our endeavors notwithstanding the opposition of our invaders. This places us in a most extraordinary and embarrassing dilemma. It would take a prophet to predict what policy America will finally adopt. I shall, however, be so bold as to offer some conjectures, which are dictated by reason and hope rather than by a plausible argument.

The position of the inhabitants in the Colombian hemisphere has been, for ages, without parallel. We were in a state *even below slavery*, and consequently suffered greater difficulty in raising ourselves to the enjoyment of liberty. Permit me to indulge in a few considerations, by way of illustration. Nations are slaves, either from the nature of their constitution, or the abuse of it; thus, a people are called slaves when the government, either by its regulations or its vices, oppresses and tramples on the rights of their subjects. By applying these principles, we shall find that America is not only deprived of liberty, but also of active tyranny and dominion. I will now explain this paradox. In absolute governments there are no limits to the authority of public functionaries. The will of the Grand Sultan, the Khan, the Bey, and other despotic sovereigns, is the supreme law, and it is arbitrarily executed by the pashas and inferior governors in Turkey and Persia, where the system of oppression is completely organized, and is submitted to by the people because of the authority from which it emanates. These subordinate officers are entrusted with the civil, military, and political administration, the collection of duties and the protection of religion. But the key difference is this: the governors of Isfahan are Persians, the viziers of the Great Lord in Turkey are Turks, and the sultans of Tartary are Tartars. In China they do not send for their mandarins, military, and literati to the country of Genghis Khan, who conquered them, even though the present race of Chinese are direct descendants of the tribes subjugated by the ancestors of the present Tartars.

With us it is quite different. We are controlled by a system which deprives us of the rights to which we are entitled, and leaves us in a sort of permanent infancy with respect to public affairs. It is for this reason that I say that we are deprived even of active tyranny because we are prohibited from serving it as functionaries. If we had been able to properly manage our domestic matters, in our internal administration, we should have learned the course and the intricacy of public negotiation. We would also have enjoyed that personal prestige which elicits from the people the respect that needs to be maintained in all revolutions.

The Americans, under the Spanish system which is perhaps now working more rigorously than ever before, occupy no other place in society than that of brutes for labour. At best we are simple consumers, clogged with repressive restrictions. For example, the prohibition of cultivating European crops, the King's monopoly of a wealth of products, the prohibition of manufactures which the Peninsula itself does not possess, the commercial restrictions on even basic necessities, the obstacles placed between provinces to keep them from intercourse and commerce. In short, if you wish to know our station, we had the bowels of the Earth to dig for gold, the plains where we could breed cattle, wildernesses to catch wild beasts for the sake of their skins, and we had the soil to produce indigo, grain, coffee, cocoa, sugar, and cotton. All this just to satisfy the needs of that avaricious nation.

Our condition is so negative that I can find nothing equal to it in any other civilized societies, although I have consulted the history of all ages, and the policy of all nations. It is an outrage and a violation of the rights of humanity to pretend that a people so blessed by nature, so extensive, rich, and populous, should be merely passive. We are, as I have just said, abstracted, and (if I may use the expression) absent, as it were, from the universe, in all that relates to the science of government and the administration of the state. We are never governors or viceroys, except in some extraordinary cases. We are archbishops and bishops very seldom; diplomats, never; military officers, only as subalterns; no magistrates, no financiers, and, indeed, scarcely merchants!

Emperor Charles V formed a pact with the discoverers, conquerors and settlers of America, which Guerra calls our social contract. The kings of Spain agreed formally and solemnly with them, that the conquest should be carried into effect at their own expense and at their own risk. They expressly prohibited any interference with the royal prerogatives, and for that reason gave them local titles as Lords of the Land. They ordered that the conquerors should take the indigenous peoples under their protection as vassals, that they should establish courts and appoint judges, that they should exercise the jurisdiction of appeals within their respective districts. All of these are set forth in the fourth volume of the Colonial Code, along with many other privileges and immunities which it would be excessive to detail. The king pledged never to disturb the American colonies, as he held no other jurisdiction over them than that of supreme domination, they being a kind of property held by the conquerors for him and his descendants. At the same time, there are *express laws, which, almost exclusively, state that the natives of America of Spanish origin should receive all civil, ecclesiastical, and financial appointments!* By this agreement the descendants of the first settlers and discoverers of America were to be the king's true representatives, and consequently the magistracy of the country is a right which belongs to them. This shows that it is a manifest violation of all existing laws and compacts for the natives to have been despoiled of that constitutional authority which was conferred by the Colonial Code.

From what I have said, it is easy to infer that America was not ready to separate from the mother country as suddenly as she did as a consequence of the illegitimate abdications at Bayonne, which had no value when applied to us because they were *contrary to our constitution*. Separation was also caused by the unjust, unlawful and unprovoked war which the Regency declared against us. There are some very excellent writings in the Spanish language where the nature of the Spanish government, their repressive and hostile decrees, and the whole course of their desperate conduct in this period is most ably treated. I content myself with referring you to the work of Señor [José María] Blanco.

The Americans have risen suddenly, without any prior knowledge, and even more remarkably, without any acquaintance with public business, which is so essentially necessary for the accomplishment of all political undertakings. Americans have suddenly advanced to the dignified eminence of being legislators, magistrates, commissioners of the national treasury, diplomats, generals, and to all the authorities, both high and low, which are necessary to form the hierarchy of an organized state.

When the French eagles destroyed the impotent government of the Peninsula, stopping only at the walls of Cádiz, we Americans were left in the state of orphans. We had first been delivered over to the mercy of a tyrant (Napoleon). Then we were flattered with a semblance of justice, and mocked with hopes, always disappointed. Finally, from a situation of uncertainty as to our future destiny, we threw ourselves into the chaos of revolution. Our first care was to provide for internal security against the machinations of the concealed enemies who were nourished in our bosoms. Our attention was next directed to the consideration of external safety, by establishing authorities to replace those we had deposed. These authorities were to guide the course of our revolution, to take advantage of the happy circumstances which allowed them to found a constitutional government, worthy of the present age, and appropriate to our situation.

All new governments first have to establish popular assemblies [*juntas*]. These assemblies then formed rules for the convocation of a congress, which finally produced important changes. Venezuela first erected a democratic and federal government, declaring the rights of man, maintaining the just balance of powers, and enacting general laws which were favourable to civil liberty, the freedom of the press, and many others. New Granada followed Venezuela's lead in political institutions and reforms, making the broadest federal system that ever existed into the fundamental basis of her constitution. She has recently improved the general executive power by making many amendments. From what I can understand, Buenos Aires and Chile have followed these examples; but as we are at so great a distance from those parts, documents so rare, and accounts so imperfect, I shall not attempt to describe the course of their transactions. There is, however, one very notable difference in a very essential point between them. Venezuela and New Granada have long ago declared their independence; it is not known whether Buenos Aires and Chile have done so yet.

Events in Mexico have been too various, complicated, rapid, and unfortunate to enable us to follow her through the revolution. We lack, moreover, documents to inform us and enable us to come to a correct judgment. From what we know, the independents of Mexico commenced their insurrection in September 1810, and a year later they had centered a government in Zitácuaro, and appointed a national *junta* under the auspices of Ferdinand VII, in whose name the functions of government were carried on. Because of the war, this *junta* was moved several times, and it is very probable that today it continues to function, though circumstances will cause it to be modified. It is said they have created a generalissimo or dictator. Some say that the illustrious general [José María] Morelos is the person, whilst others speak of the celebrated general [Ignacio López] Rayón. What is certain is that one of these great men, or perhaps both of them separately, exercise the supreme authority in those parts. In March 1812 this government, then resident at Zultepec, presented a plan of peace and war to the viceroy, which was conceived with the profoundest wisdom. In it they claimed the rights of citizens and established principles of incontrovertible strength. They proposed that the rights of America should be respected, or at least that the war should not be conducted with blood and fire, or with carnage unknown even amongst barbarians. It appears that for convenience, and the appearance of submission to the king, the constitution of the monarchy has been preserved. It seems that the National *Junta* is *absolute* in the exercise of its legislative, executive, and judicial functions, and the number of its members is very limited.

The occurrences in Terra Firma [the South American mainland] have proved to us that purely representative institutions are not suited to our character, customs, and understandings. In Caracas party spirit grew out of societies, assemblies, and popular elections, and this led us back to a state of servitude. And thus Venezuela, which has been the republic among us most advanced in its political establishments, affords us a striking example of the inefficacy of a democratic and federal system of government in our unsettled condition. In New Granada the excessive authority of the provincial governments, and the want of vigour and capacity in the central government, have reduced that beautiful country to the state in which we now see her. For this reason civil war has always raged there, and her enemies have maintained themselves against all probability. Until our patriots acquire those talents and political virtues which distinguish our North American brethren, I am very much afraid that our popular systems, far from being favourable to us, will cause our ruin. Unhappily for us, we appear to be very distant from the requisite perfection in these good qualities, whilst we are infected with the vices we contracted under the dominion of the Spanish nation.

"It is more difficult," says Montesquieu, "to rescue a nation from slavery, than to subject a free nation." This truth is established by the history of all ages, wherein we see many instances of free nations submitting to a yoke, but very few of enslaved nations recovering their liberty. Notwithstanding this conviction, the inhabitants of this continent have displayed the desire to form liberal and even perfect institutions, no doubt from the influence of that instinct which all men possess of aspiring to the greatest possible happiness, and which can only be obtained in those civil societies, founded on the grand basis of justice, liberty, and equality. But will we be able to manage the difficulties of a truly balanced Republic? Can you conceive that a people only just released from their chains could fly up at once into the sphere of liberty, without their wings coming off like those of Icarus, causing them to fall back into the abyss? Such a miracle is inconceivable and unprecedented. Therefore there is no reasonable argument which could support such a hope.

More than anyone, I wish to see the greatest nation in the world formed in America. Although I desire, and indeed anticipate the perfection of government in my country, I cannot persuade myself that this new world will be ruled by one great republic. As it is impossible, I do not wish for it, and am still less anxious for one universal monarchy in America, because that project, without being useful, is equally impossible. The abuses which currently exist could not be reformed, and our regeneration would be unavailing. These American States require the care of paternal governments, that the sores and wounds inflicted by despotism and war may be healed. The metropolis, for example, might be Mexico, which is the only fit place from its intrinsic power, and without that, in fact, there can be no metropolis. Even if the metropolis was to be the isthmus of Panama, the central point of this vast continent, would not the territorial extremes continue in their state of indifference, and even in their present disorder? For one government alone to animate, give life to, and appropriate all the resources of public prosperity, for it to correct, illustrate, and perfect the new world, it would indeed require the faculties of a divinity, and the enlightenment and virtues of all mankind!

That party spirit which now afflicts our provinces would then burn with greater fury, from the want of a sufficient power to restrain it. Moreover, the leaders of the chief cities would not permit the domination of the metropolitans, but would consider them as so many tyrants, and their jealousy would carry them so far as to compare them with the odious Spaniards. In brief, such a monarchy would be like a ponderous colossus, which its own weight would shake down upon the smallest convulsion.

M. de Pradt has very wisely divided America into fifteen or seventeen distinct states, independent of each other, and each governed by its own sovereign. I agree with him in his division, because America consists of seventeen nations, but with regard to his governments, although easier to achieve, American monarchies are less useful. I will give my reasons. The interest of a republic, when well understood, is confined to preservation, prosperity, and glory. Republican liberty is precisely the opposite of dominion. There is no stimulus to excite republicans to sacrifice their means to extend their boundaries, or for the sole purpose of inducing their neighbours to participate in a liberal constitution. They acquire no right and no advantage by conquests, unless by following the example of Rome their conquests are reduced to *colonies* or made *allies*. Such maxims and examples are in direct opposition to the principles of justice in republican systems. What is more, they are in manifest opposition to the interests of the people; for when a state becomes too extensive, either in itself or from its dependencies, it falls into confusion, converts its free form into a sort of tyranny, abandons those principles which ought to preserve it, and at length degenerates into despotism. The essence of small republics is *permanency*, and that of great ones is *changeability*, but always inclined to dominion. Of the first, almost all have been of long duration; of the second, Rome alone maintained itself for ages, but that was because Rome alone was a republic, and the rest of her territories were not so, and were governed by different laws and institutions.

A King's policy is very different, as his constant attention is directed to increasing his possessions, his riches, and his prerogatives. And rightly enough, because his authority increases with these acquisitions, as much with respect to his neighbors as to his own subjects, who fear in him a power as formidable as his empire, and which is preserved by war and conquests. For these reasons I think that Americans, desirous of peace, sciences, arts, commerce, and agriculture, would prefer republics to monarchies; and it occurs to me that this wish corresponds with the views which Europe has with respect to us.

As a popular and representative framework I do not approve of the federal system because it is too perfect. It requires virtues and political talents which we do not possess. For the same reason I disapprove of the monarchy composed of aristocracy and democracy, which has raised England to fortune and splendour. Not being able, amongst republics and monarchies, to select a perfect and accommodating system, we must content ourselves with avoiding demagoguery, anarchy and oppressive tyranny. We must seek a medium between extremes which would lead us to dishonour and unhappiness. I will now explain the result of my speculations as to the best system for America. It is not perhaps the best, but that which will be most acceptable to her.

From the situation, riches, population and character of the Mexicans, I imagine they will first establish a representative republic, in which the executive branch will possess great power, which will be centered in an individual, who, if he discharges his functions with diligence and justice, it is natural to suppose that he will preserve a lasting authority. If his incapacity or violent administration should excite any popular commotion that may prove successful, executive power will disperse into and become an assembly. If the more powerful party should be military or aristocratic, they would probably found a monarchy, which at first might be constitutional and limited, but which would inevitably afterwards decline into an unlimited one. It must be admitted that there is nothing more difficult in political order than the preservation of a mixed monarchy, and it is equally true that only a patriotic nation like the English could submit to the authority of a king and maintain the spirit of liberty under the dominion of a sceptre and a crown.

The provinces on the isthmus of Panama, as far as Guatemala, will perhaps form a league. This magnificent position between the two great seas may in time become the emporium of the universe. Her canals will shorten the distances in the world; will extend the commercial intercourse of Europe, Asia, and America, and will bring to that happy region the products of the four quarters of the globe. Only here can the *capital of the earth* be fixed, as Constantine says Byzantium was to the old world.

New Granada will unite with Venezuela, if they agree on the form of a central republic, and Maracaibo, from its situation and advantages, will be the capital.[7] This government will imitate the English, with one difference. In place of a king they will have an executive power which will be elected, perhaps for a life term, but certainly not hereditary. They will have a hereditary legislative senate or house, which, in tempestuous times, may interpose between the commotions of the people and the acts of the government. They will have a legislative body called by the free elective franchise, and without any other restrictions than those imposed on the English House of Commons. This constitution will be composed of all forms, but will not, I hope, participate in all vices. *As this is my native country, I have an undeniable right to wish her what, in my opinion, may be most to her advantage.*

It is possible that New Granada may not agree to recognize a central government, as she is extremely partial to federalism. In such case she may perhaps establish a state by herself, which, if it should last, will be very happy from the very great and various advantages she possesses.

We know little of the opinions which prevail in Buenos Aires, Chile, and Peru. But judging from that little, and from appearances, it is fair to presume that in Buenos Aires there will be a central government in which the military will take the lead, on account of internal divisions and external wars. This constitution will necessarily degenerate into an oligarchy or monarchy, under certain restrictions, the denomination of which no one can guess.

The kingdom of Chile is intended by nature, from its geographical nature, from the innocent and virtuous customs of the inhabitants, and from the example of her neighbours, the fierce republicans of Araucania, to enjoy the blessings which emanate from the just and moderate laws of a republic. If in any part of America that system of government should continue for any time, I am inclined to think it will be in Chile. The spirit of liberty has there never been extinguished; the vices of Europe and Asia will come very late, and perhaps never to corrupt the pure morals of that part of the earth. The territory has clear limits, and will always be beyond the reach of the contagious influence of the rest of mankind. Her laws, customs, and manners will never be polluted, and she will preserve her uniformity in political and religious opinions. In a word, Chile can be free![8]

Peru, on the other hand, is afflicted with two things which are enemies to all just and liberal regimens—gold and slavery! The first corrupts every thing; the second is inherently corrupt. The soul of a stag seldom gets to enjoy rational liberty: he becomes fierce or gets trapped in snares. Although these rules may be applicable to all America, they are still more so to Lima, because of the opinions which I have already expressed, and because of the cooperation with which they assisted their masters against their own brethren, the heroes of Quito, Chile, and Buenos Aires. It is an axiom that those who aspire to obtain their freedom should at least attempt to gain it. I am of the opinion that the higher classes in Lima would not tolerate democracy, nor the slaves and *pardos* an aristocracy. The first would prefer the tyranny of one individual, to be exempted from oppressive persecutions, and if possible to establish a regular order of things. I am very much afraid that the Peruvians will scarcely succeed in their efforts to recover their independence.

From all that has been said, we may be led to the following conclusions. The American provinces are now struggling for emancipation. They will in the end be successful. Some will be constituted in a regular manner, as federal or central republics. The extensive territories will undoubtedly found monarchies, and some will destroy their principles as well in the present contest as in future revolutions. One great republic is impossible, one great monarchy very difficult to consolidate.

It is a most magnificent idea to form the new world into one great nation, linked together by one great chain. Professing the same religion, language, origin, and customs, it would seem that it should have but one government to join the different states that may be formed. But this is impossible, because America is divided by distant regions, various situations, contending interests, and dissimilar characters.

How sublime it would be if the isthmus of Panama should become to us what Corinth was to the Greeks. I hope that some day we shall have the happiness of installing the representatives of republics, kingdoms, and empires in one august congress, and of treating and discussing great and interesting questions of peace and war with nations of the other three parts of the globe. This sort of body may very possibly occur during some happy stage of our regeneration. Any other expectation is impractical, for instance that of the Abbé de Saint-Pierre, who with commendable delirium conceived the idea of a European congress which would decide on the fate and interests of these nations.

Returning to your letter, you remark that

important and happy changes may very frequently be produced by individual exertions. The Americans have a tradition, which relates that when Quetzalcoatl, the Hermes or Buddha of South America, resigned his power and abandoned them, he promised that after a specified time he would return to them, reestablish their government, and restore their happiness. This tradition encourages the belief that he will shortly reappear. Consider, Sir, what effect would be produced by the appearance of an individual among them, who would exemplify the character of Quetzalcoatl, the Buddha of the Mexican rainforest, of whom other nations have said so much? Do you not think it would incline all parties to unite? And is not union all that is necessary to put them in a condition to expel the Spanish troops, to enable them to establish a powerful empire, with a free government and liberal laws?

I agree with you that individual efforts can have general effects, particularly during revolutions. But Quetzalcoatl, the hero and prophet of Anahuac, is not the one capable of bringing about the prodigious benefits which you contemplate. This personage is very superficially and not very advantageously known to the people of Mexico, for such is the fate of the vanquished, even gods. Historians and literati have carefully confined themselves to the investigation of his origin, his mission, whether true or false, his prophecies, and the termination of his career. It is disputed whether he was an apostle of Christ or a pagan. Some suppose that the meaning of his name, both in the Mexican and Chinese languages, is Saint Thomas. Some say that it means a feathered snake and others that he is the famous prophet of Yucatan, Chilam-Cambal. In a word, most of the Mexican authors, polemicists, and profane historians have engaged at some stage with the question of the true character of Quetzalcoatl. Acosta says that Quetzalcoatl established a religion, and that its rights, dogmas, and mysteries bore a remarkable affinity to that of Christ, and perhaps more than any other resembles it. Notwithstanding this, many Catholic writers deny that he was a true prophet and have refused to recognize him as Saint Thomas, as other celebrated authors maintain. The general belief is that Quetzalcoatl was a divine legislator amongst the pagan tribes of Anahuac, of whom the great Montezuma was the Emperor, and that Montezuma derived his authority from Quetzalcoatl. From this it is to be inferred that the Mexicans would not be disposed to follow a heathen Quetzalcoatl, even if he should make his appearance under the most identical and favourable circumstances, because they profess the most intolerant religion of all!

Happily the promoters of Mexican independence have taken good advantage of this fanaticism by proclaiming the celebrated Virgin of Guadalupe to be the Queen of the Patriots, invoking her in all their sacred appeals, and representing her on their flags. By these means political enthusiasm has become united with religion, and producing a most vehement fervour for the sacred cause of liberty. The reverence with which the Virgin of Guadalupe's image is received in Mexico is superior to the most exalted feeling which the most fortunate prophet could inspire.

On the other hand, the season of these heavenly visitations is past. Even if Americans were more superstitious than they really are, they would not give their faith to the doctrines of an impostor, who would be considered as a schismatic, or as the Antichrist announced in our religion.[9]

Union is certainly what we need most in order to complete our regeneration. However, our division is not surprising, for this is the distinguishing feature of all civil wars formed between two parties: the friends of the status quo, and the reformers. The first are usually the most numerous, because the empire of custom generally produces obedience to constituted authorities; the last are always less in number, but more arduous and enthusiastic. Thus it happens that physical power is balanced with moral force, and the contest is prolonged while the result is uncertain. Fortunately, in our case the people have followed the intelligent cause.

I will tell you what will enable us to expel the Spaniards and to found a free government. We need unity to be sure; but that unity will not be the result of divine intervention, but rather by energetic measures and well-directed efforts. America is left to herself, abandoned by all nations, isolated in the centre of the universe, with no diplomatic relations or military support, and we fight against Spain, which has more implements of warfare than we can possibly obtain.

When successes are doubtful, when the state is weak, and when hopes are remote, all men vacillate, opinions divide and passions become inflamed. All this is encouraged by our enemies so that they may succeed with greater ease. As soon as we become strong, and under the auspices of a liberal nation that will afford us protection, we shall be united.

We shall then follow that majestic march towards the grand state of prosperity which is destined for America. Then the sciences and arts, which were born in the east and then enlightened Europe, will fly to free Colombia, which will give them shelter and asylum.

Such, Sir, are the observations and thoughts which I have the honor of submitting to you, so that you may correct and improve them according to their merit. And I beg you to believe me that I have replied in this way more out of politeness than because I believe myself capable of educating you on the subject. I am, &c. &c.

Simón Bolívar
Kingston, Jamaica, 6 September 1815

NOTES

1 The letter was first published in English in Kingston in the *Jamaica Quarterly Journal and Literary Gazette* in July 1818 under the title "General Bolívar's Letter to a Friend, on the Subject of South-America's Independence.—*(Translated from the Spanish)*." The original Spanish manuscript does not survive, though a handwritten draft of the English version does. Correspondence from the period suggests that Bolívar's close friend, the Canadian-born John Robertson, did the translation in a hurry, which may account for the many literal translations from Spanish to English which lose much (if not all) of their meaning in the process. The present revision aims to remedy these flaws while allowing the reader to focus on the radical and incisive nature of Bolívar's ideas in their original form. For a comprehensive survey of the Jamaica Letter and its origins, see Tomás Polanco Alcántara, *Simón Bolívar: Ensayo de una interpretación biográfica a través de sus documentos* (Caracas: E.G., 1993), pp.272-5. On Robertson, see Carlos Pi Sunyer, *El General Juan Robertson: Un procer de la independencia* (Caracas: Editorial Arte, 1971).

2 Antonio de Herrera y Tordesillas (1559–1625) and Antonio de Solís y Rivadeneyra (1610–86) were amongst the main Spanish chroniclers of the conquest and colonization of the Americas.

3 Bolívar repeatedly returned to the metaphor of Spain as a wicked stepmother *(madrastra)* rather than mother country *(madre patria)*. For

an excellent discussion of the place of gender in Bolívar's writings see Catherine Davies, Claire Brewster and Hillary Owen, *South American Independence: Gender, Politics, Text* (Liverpool: Liverpool University Press, 2006).

4 This paragraph was omitted from the English original and has been inserted based on Lewis Bertrand's translation.

5 Here Robertson's translation lacks two sentences (on General Pablo Morillo's planned reconquest of New Granada) which are present in most versions of the Jamaica Letter. Similar omissions occur on several occasions throughout the text. In this translation I have generally followed Robertson's lead, which privileges brevity and clarity over length. Many of the extra sections were added at later stages of composition/translation/publication. Fornoff's translation in the OUP edition retains most of the additions. On the various versions of the letter, see *Escritos,* Vol.8.

6 Bolívar is referring to articles published by his correspondent, the English journalist William Walton.

7 Later versions of the letter include an alternative suggestion that the capital might be inland, on the border between Venezuela and New Granada, and that it might be named after Las Casas. In effect, the republic's temporary capital was moved to this region in 1821 during the meetings of the Congress of Cúcuta, but after that it shifted definitively to Bogotá.

8 Bolívar here invokes the image of the undefeated Araucanian Indians of southern and central Chile, who successfully resisted Spanish attempts at conquest. The independent Chilean state only succeeded in "pacifying" the Araucanians (now known as the Mapuche) in the late nineteenth century.

9 On this point see Olivia Harris's interesting article "The Coming of the White People: Reflections on the Mythologising of History in Latin America," *Bulletin of Latin American Research* 14:1 (1995) pp. 9–24.

7

DECREE FOR THE EMANCIPATION OF SLAVES

2 June 1816

During his exile in Haiti, Bolívar received support and material assistance from the Haitian President Alexandre Pétion. In return, Bolívar pledged to free all slaves upon his return to Venezuela, a still radical step at the time. Though slavery was abolished in Haiti in 1804, the institution was only disbanded in the British Empire in 1834, the USA in 1865, in the remaining Spanish colonies in 1886 and in Brazil in 1888. This document shows Bolívar fulfilling his promise in the Venezuelan coastal lands around Carúpano.

To the Inhabitants of Río Caribe, Carúpano, and Cariaco, Greetings:

Considering that justice, policy, and the country imperiously demand the inalienable rights of nature, I have decided to formally decree absolute freedom for the slaves who have groaned under the Spanish yoke during the three previous centuries.[1] Considering that the Republic needs the services of all her children, we must impose on these new citizens the following conditions:

Article 1—Every healthy man between the ages of fourteen and sixty shall appear in the parish church of his district to enlist under the flag of Venezuela, within twenty-four hours of the publication of this decree.

Article 2—Old men, women, children, and invalids shall be exempt from this day forth from military service and exempt as well from any domestic or field service in which they were previously employed for the benefit of their masters.

Article 3—The new citizen who refuses to bear arms in fulfillment of the sacred duty to defend his freedom shall be subject to servitude, not only for himself but also for his children under the age of fourteen, his wife, and his aged parents.

Article 4—The relatives of the military occupied in the army of liberation shall enjoy the rights of citizens and the absolute freedom granted to them by this decree in the name of the Republic of Venezuela.

The present regulation shall have the force of law and be faithfully executed by the Republican Authorities of Río Caribe, Carúpano, and Cariaco.

Signed into law in the General Headquarters of Carúpano on 2 June 1816.

Simón Bolívar
Commander in Chief and Captain General of the Armies of Venezuela and New Granada, etc.

NOTE

1 Note that at this stage, Bolívar limited himself to freeing the slaves in this region on the condition that they joined his army. At no point was he in favour of the total unconditional or immediate abolition of slavery, which was only finally eradicated in Venezuela in 1854. See John V. Lombardi, *The Decline and Abolition of Negro Slavery 1820–1854* (Westport, CN: Greenwood Press, 1971) and Miguel Acosta Saignes, *Vida de los esclavos negros en Venezuela* (Caracas: Hespérides, 1967).

8

MANIFESTO ON THE
EXECUTION OF MANUEL PIAR

17 October 1817

*When Bolívar returned to Venezuela from his Haitian exile in 1816
he attempted to convince the military leaders who had continued the
fight in his absence that they should recognize his supreme authority.
Manuel Piar reluctantly gave in to Bolívar's power and support, and
resigned his commissions, but he was accused of fomenting disobedience
to Bolívar's rule, tried, and sentenced to death. Bolívar approved the
death sentence and then felt obliged to publish this manifesto explaining
his decision.*

To the Soldiers of the Liberating Army:

Soldiers! Yesterday was a day of sorrow for my heart. General Piar
was executed for his crimes against the country, for conspiracy
and desertion. A just and legal tribunal has pronounced the
sentence against that unfortunate citizen who, intoxicated by
the favours of fortune and to satisfy his ambition, tried to bury
the country amid her ruins. General Piar truly had rendered
important service to the Republic, and though the course of
his conduct had always been factious, his services had been
rewarded generously by the government of Venezuela.

For a leader who had obtained the highest military rank, there was nothing left to aspire to. Prior to his rebellion, the second highest authority of the republic, which had been vacated due to the dissidence of General [Santiago] Mariño, was about to be conferred on him; but this general, who aspired only to the supreme command, contrived the most atrocious plot a perverse soul can conceive. Piar sought not only civil war but anarchy and the most inhuman sacrifice of his fellow soldiers and brothers.[1]

Soldiers! You know this. Equality, liberty, and independence are our motto. Has not humankind regained its rights through our laws? Have our arms not destroyed the chains of slaves? Have not the odious differences between classes and colours been abolished forever? Has it not been ordered that the wealth of the nation be fairly distributed among you? Do not fortune, knowledge, and glory await you? Are your merits not richly, or at least fairly, rewarded? What then could General Piar have wanted on your behalf? Are you not equal, free, independent, happy, and honoured? Could Piar have secured greater good for you? No, no, no! Piar was digging the grave of the republic with his own hands and was about to bury in it the lives, properties, and honour of the brave defenders of Venezuela's freedom, of her sons, wives, and fathers.

Heaven looked with horror on this cruel patricide. Heaven delivered him to the rigours of the law. Heaven ordained that a man who had offended divinity and the human race should no longer profane the earth or be further tolerated after his infamous crime.

Soldiers! Heaven keeps vigil over your welfare, and the government that is your father watches over you. Your general, who is your companion in arms, and who has always marched at your head and shared your dangers and hardships as well as your triumphs, puts his trust in you. Therefore, put your trust in him, confident that he loves you more than if he were your father or your son.

Simón Bolívar
Supreme Commander of the Republic of Venezuela, etc., etc.
General Headquarters in Angostura, 17 October 1817

NOTE

1 Recently historians have stressed Manuel Piar's ethnicity as one of
the motivations for the execution, though it was referred to only
implicitly by Bolívar. Piar was a *pardo,* the son of a white Canarian
father and black mother from Curacao. See especially Aline Helg,
"Simón Bolívar and the Spectre of Pardocracia: José Padilla in Post-
Independence Cartagena," *Journal of Latin American Studies,* 35:3
(2003), p.462. In this manifesto, Bolívar makes no mention at all
of questions of race or ethnicity; instead he casts Piar's rebellion in
the language of insubordination to Bolívar as the *padre de la patria.*

9

DECLARATION OF ANGOSTURA

20 November 1818

In late 1818, rumours spread that Spain was raising an army and naval expedition to crush the independence movements in Venezuela. Britain and Spain had been involved in lengthy negotiations over any mediating role that Britain might play. Faced with the possibility that Britain might get tired of wrangling and bow to Spanish demands, Bolívar issued this forthright statement of Venezuelan strength. His fluent prose set out a clear and confident vision of Venezuelan liberty, which would be realized through military victory the next year. Britain never played a formal role in negotiating an end to the conflict.

Considering that when the Spanish government requests the mediation of the major powers in its effort to reconcile and reestablish its authority over the free and independent people of America, it is urgent that we convey to the world Venezuela's feelings and decision.

That even though these feelings and that decision were embodied in the establishment of the Republic on 5 July 1811 and more specifically since the very first announcements of the proposition of the government of Madrid, it is the obligation of those representing the national government to reiterate them, giving them formal expression in solemn and legal terms.

That we are obliged to make this frank and clear declaration not only out of respect and consideration for the major powers but even more urgently to calm the spirits of the citizens of Venezuela.

Having convened a national meeting of all the civil and military authorities, including the Council of State, the Supreme Court of Justice, the governor, the vicar general of this vacant diocese, and the general staff of the armed forces, and having examined with great care the conduct of the Spanish government, we have borne in mind:

1. that the idea of cordial reconciliation was never a consideration of the Spanish government.
2. that though Great Britain twice proposed such a reconciliation from the first days of our disagreements, Spain, in defiance of all parties, rejected it.[1]
3. that even while efforts at reconciliation were being negotiated, she blocked our ports, sent armies against us, and conspired to destroy us.
4. that having subjected Venezuela to terms of solemn capitulation, no sooner had we put down our arms than she violated every article of that armistice, sacrificing thousands of citizens whose rights had been guaranteed.
5. that waging against us a war to the death without respect for sex, age, or condition, she broke every social bond and aroused our just and implacable hatred.
6. that this hatred has been exacerbated by the atrocities she has committed and by the bad faith she has shown us at every juncture.
7. that all America, and very particularly Venezuela, is thoroughly convinced of the absolute impossibility that Spain could ever recover her authority on this continent.
8. that all America is now satisfied of her power and her resources: she is fully aware of her natural advantages and

means of defense and secure in her conviction that no power on earth can ever bind her to Spain again.

9. that even if there were such a power, she is resolved to perish rather than be subjected again to a government of blood, fire, and devastation.

10. that having found ourselves in possession of the freedom and independence for which nature destined us, and which even the laws of Spain and the examples of her history authorized us to seize by force of arms, as we have in fact done, it would be an act of deranged stupidity to bow down to the Spanish government no matter what the conditions.

Due to all these considerations, the government of Venezuela, interpreter of the national will and purpose, has seen fit to proclaim to the world the following declaration:

1. that the Republic of Venezuela, by divine and human right, is emancipated from the Spanish nation and constituted as an independent, free, and sovereign state.

2. that Spain has no right to reclaim dominion over her, nor does Europe have the right to attempt to subject her to the Spanish government.

3. that Venezuela has not requested, nor will she ever request, incorporation into the Spanish nation.

4. that she has not requested the mediation of the major powers to seek reconciliation with Spain.

5. that she will never deal with Spain, in peace or war, except on terms of equality, as is the mutual practice of all nations.

6. that she only desires the mediation of foreign powers to exert their good offices on behalf of humanity, inviting Spain to draft and sign a treaty of peace and friendship

with the Venezuelan nation, recognizing and dealing with her as a free, independent, and sovereign state.

7. and that, finally, the Republic of Venezuela declares that she has been engaged in a struggle for her rights since 19 April 1810, shedding the blood of most of her sons, sacrificing her wealth, her pleasures, and everything that men hold dear and sacred, in her effort to recover her sovereign rights, and that to retain her integrity, as Divine Providence has ordained, the people of Venezuela are resolved to bury themselves alive amid the ruins if Spain, or Europe, or the world seeks to subject her to the Spanish yoke.

Presented, signed by my hand, sealed with the provisional seal of the Republic, and countersigned by the secretary of state in the Palace of Government in Angostura on 20 November 1818, the eighth year of independence.

Simón Bolívar
Supreme Commander of the Republic of Venezuela, etc.
Angostura, 20 November 1818

For His Excellency the Supreme Commander, the Secretary of State, Pedro Briceño Méndez

NOTE

1 For a retrospective discussion of proposals for and negotiation over British mediation see John Rydjord, "British Mediation between Spain and her Colonies," *Hispanic American Historical Review,* 21 (1941) pp.29–50.

Part II

ESTABLISHING COLOMBIA

10

ANGOSTURA ADDRESS

15 February 1819

In order to give the former colonies a louder voice on the international stage, Bolívar proclaimed the independence of Colombia, to consist of the former territories of the viceroyalty of New Granada, the captaincy-general of Venezuela and the Presidency of Quito. Spain retained formal control of almost the entire territory as the Congress of Angostura met, theoretically representing the whole region but in reality dominated by Venezuelans due to obvious reasons of communication and distance. Bolívar made this speech at the inauguration of the Congress on 15 February 1819, reflecting on the nature of Venezuelan society and clearly setting out his thoughts on the type of government most appropriate for the new republic. His wide-ranging comparisons to Athens, Sparta, Rome, the United States, China and Great Britain reveal Bolívar's extensive learning, his global vision and his constant efforts to innovate rather than replicate political models from elsewhere.

I account myself one of the more fortunate men, in having the honor of reuniting the representatives of Venezuela in this august congress; the only source of legitimate authority, the deposit of the sovereign will, and the arbiter of the nation's fate.[1]

In delivering back to the representatives of the people the supreme power entrusted to me, I satisfy the desires of my own heart, and calm the wishes of my fellow citizens and of future generations, who expect much from your wisdom, rectitude, and prudence. In fulfilling this delightful duty, I free myself from the boundless authority which oppresses me, and also from the unlimited responsibility which weighs on my feeble hands.

Only an imperative necessity, united to a strongly expressed desire on the part of the people, could have induced me to assume the dreadful and dangerous office of dictator, supreme chief of the republic. Now, however, I breathe again as I give up this authority which, with such great risk, difficulty and toil, I have maintained amidst the most horrible calamities as ever afflicted a social body.

In the epoch during which I presided over the Republic, it was not merely a political storm that raged, in a sanguinary war, in a time of popular anarchy, but the tempest of the desert, a whirlwind of every disorganized element, the bursting of an infernal torrent that overwhelmed the land of Venezuela. A man! And such a man as I am! What bounds, what resistance, could he oppose to such furious devastation! Amidst that sea of woes and afflictions, I was nothing more than the miserable sport of the revolutionary hurricane, driven to and fro like the wild bird of the ocean. I could do neither good nor evil; an irresistible power above all human control directed the march of our fortunes, and for me to pretend to have been the protagonist would be unjust and would claim for me importance that I do not merit. Do you wish to know the sources from which those events came, and the origin of our present situation? Then consult the annals of Spain, of America, and of Venezuela; examine the laws of the Indies, the conduct of your ancient governors, the influence of religion, and of foreign dominion; observe the first acts of the republican government, the ferocity of our enemies, and the national character. I again repeat that I cannot consider myself more than the mere instrument of the great forces which have acted on our country. My life, my conduct, and all my actions, public and private, are however before the people—and representatives, it is your duty to judge them. I submit the history of my command to your impartial decision, and I have nothing to add to explain my actions; I have already said enough in my defense. Should I merit your approbation, I shall have acquired the sublime title of a *good citizen*, preferred by me to that of *liberator*, bestowed on me by Venezuela, to that of *perfecter*, given by Cundinamarca, and to all others the universe could confer.

Legislators! I place Venezuela's supreme command in your hands. It is your solemn duty to dedicate yourselves to the happiness of the Republic. In your hands lies the balance of our destiny and the measure of our glory. Your decisions will confirm the decrees which establish our liberty.

The supreme chief of the Republic is, at this moment, nothing more than a simple citizen. He wishes to remain as such until his death. He will, however, serve with the armies of Venezuela, as long as an enemy treads her soil.

Our country has many deserving sons capable of governing her. Many here in this assembly, and many outside its walls, have the necessary talents, virtues, experience and other requisites for good governance. Citizens are to be found who, at all times, have given proofs of their valour in encountering dangers, of their prudence in eschewing them, and in short of the art of governing themselves, and governing others. These illustrious individuals certainly merit the votes of congress, and to occupy the position from which I have just definitively resigned forever.

The continuation of authority in the same individual has frequently proved the ruin of democratic governments. Repeated elections are essential in popular systems, for nothing is so dangerous as to allow power to remain a long time vested in one citizen; the people become accustomed to obey, and he to command, and this gives rise to usurpation and tyranny. A strict jealousy is the guarantee of republican liberty, and the citizens of Venezuela ought to fear with the greatest justice, that the same magistrate, who has governed them for a length of time, may do so for ever.

I hope that by acting thus in the best interests of my country's liberty, I may deserve to be called one of her most patriotic sons.

Permit me, sirs, with the frankness of a true republican, to lay before you a respectful outline of the project of a constitution, which I take the liberty of offering, in testimony of my sincerity and candour. I believe that I have the right to be heard by the representatives of the people in the name of our common security. I am well aware that your wisdom needs no advice, and I am moreover aware that my project may appear erroneous and impracticable; but, sirs, accept with kindness this work, which is, I do assure you, rather a tribute of my sincere submission to the congress than the production of presumptuous levity. Your installation as a congress marks the creation of a new political body, even the beginning of an entirely new society, which finds itself surrounded by unprecedented and difficult circumstances. One citizen's call may at least be able to alert you to some hidden dangers.

By casting a glance at our past, we can make out the origins of the Republic of Venezuela.

The separation of America from the Spanish Monarchy resembles the state of the Roman Empire, when that enormous structure fell to pieces in the midst of the ancient world. Every piece then formed an independent Nation in accordance with its situation and interests, as now, but with the difference that those countries were able to return to their original principles. We do not retain vestiges of what we were in other times; we are not Europeans, we are not Indians, but a middle race between the indigenous peoples and the Spaniards. Americans by birth and Europeans in rights, we are placed in an extraordinary predicament. We have to maintain ourselves in the country where we were born, against the efforts of the original invaders, while at the same time disputing with the natives our privilege of possession. Our situation is thus more extraordinary and complicated that that faced by the heirs to the Roman Empire.

Furthermore, it is even more difficult for us to establish our liberties, as up to now our political existence has been virtually nil. We were even more degraded than slaves. Without an active or domineering tyranny to rail against we lived purely passive lives, without indignation, without resistance and without freedom.

Permit me to explain this paradox. In the exercise of authorized absolute power, there are no limits. The despot's will is the supreme law, which is arbitrarily carried out by subalterns who participate in the organized oppression in proportion to the authority they hold. These inferiors are entrusted with all functions, civil, political, military and religious. America received all these from Spain and was not permitted to share in the administration of her domestic concerns and arrangements. There was no active tyranny in America.

This abject state of affairs rendered it impossible for us to be acquainted with the course of public affairs. We therefore lacked the public respect which the show of authority commands in the people's eyes, and which is of such importance in great revolutions. I say again, we were isolated and absent from the world and science of government. The people of America, bound with the triple yoke of ignorance, tyranny and vice, could not acquire either knowledge, power or virtue.

Pupils of such pernicious masters—the lessons we received, and the examples we followed—were the most destructive. We were governed more by deceit and treachery than by force, and were degraded more by vice than by superstition. Slavery is the daughter of darkness, and an ignorant person is generally the blind instrument of his own ruin. Ambition and intrigue take advantage of the credulity and inexperience of men totally unacquainted with every principle of political and civil economy. The uninformed adopt as realities what are mere illusions, they mistake licentiousness for liberty, treachery for patriotism, and revenge for justice.

If a corrupt people should win its freedom it will surely soon lose it again. The light of experience will be employed in vain in showing that happiness consists in the practice of virtue and that the government of laws is more powerful than that of tyrants. But these laws are more valuable, and all should submit to their wholesome severity. The pillars of the law are constituted by good morals and not force. The exercise of justice is the exercise of liberty.

Thus, legislators, your undertaking is so much the more laborious, as you have to deal with men corrupted by the illusions of error, and by noxious incitements. Liberty, says Rousseau, is a succulent food, but difficult to digest. Our weak and feeble fellow citizens will have to increase in strength of mind in a very great degree, before they can be permitted to digest freedom's wholesome food. With their limbs numbed by shackles, and their eyesight weakened by dungeon's darkness, are they capable of marching with firm steps towards the august temple of liberty? Are they capable of supporting its splendid rays? Or of breathing freely the pure ether that reigns there?

Legislators! Consider well the matter in hand. Keep in mind that you are about to form a fundamental code for an incipient people. If you pitch the basis of the structure to what can be reasonably expected, the people may rise to heights that nature allows. However, if you do not learn the important lessons of Venezuela's experience, if you do not employ prudence and wisdom to shape the government's nature and form in the interests of the people's happiness, then you can be sure that slavery will be the result.

History presents us with an immense variety of governments to choose from. If you can recall the nations which have figured most conspicuously in the history of the world, you will sadly note that almost the whole earth has been, and is, the victim of its government. You will find many systems for governing men, but most for oppressing them. This would be truly shocking if we had not become accustomed to such a revolting spectacle, to seeing our docile species grazing on the surface of the globe, like cattle, destined for the use of their cruel masters. It is true that nature endows us at birth with an inclination to liberty, but whether out of sloth or something else, it is a fact that our freedom remains still and quiet under the trammels imposed upon her. In contemplating our freedom thus prostituted, it would appear that most of mankind does believe in that humiliating maxim, which says that it is more difficult to maintain the equilibrium of liberty than to sustain the weight of tyranny. Oh God, if only this unnatural maxim was false! Oh God, if only this fact had not been sanctioned by man's indolence with the respect to his most sacred rights.

Many ancient and modern nations have shaken off oppression, but few of them have known how to enjoy a few precious moments of freedom. Soon enough they have returned to their former political vices, as the people bring tyranny on themselves more frequently than government. The submissive habit renders them insensible to the charms of honour and national prosperity, and leads them to disregard the glory of being free under the protection of laws dictated by their own will. This dreadful truth is proclaimed by the history of the world.

Only democracy is compatible with complete liberty, in my opinion. But what democratic government was ever able to unite power, prosperity and permanency at the same time? On the contrary, aristocracy and monarchy have long established great and powerful empires. What government is more ancient than that of China? What republic has exceeded in duration those of Sparta and Venice? Did not the Roman Empire conquer the world? Did not monarchy exist in France for fourteen centuries? What state is more powerful than Great Britain? The governments, however, of those nations, were either aristocratic or monarchical.

Notwithstanding such painful reflections, my mind is filled with joy at the great progress made by our republic in its glorious career—loving what is useful, animated by what is just, and aspiring to what is perfect. Venezuela, on separating from Spain, recovered her independence and liberty, her equality and her national sovereignty. Constituting herself into a democratic republic, she prohibited monarchy, distinctions, nobility, charters, and privileges. She declared the rights of man, and freedom of action, freedom of thought, freedom of expression and freedom to write. Those liberal acts, and the purity which engendered them, cannot be praised highly enough. Venezuela's First Congress embossed the majesty of the people in indelible print in the annals of our legislation, when it passed the social decree which is most capable of leading to happiness of the nation. I need every feeling in my mind to fully appreciate the supreme virtue embodied in that immortal code of our rights and laws. But yet . . . how can I express this? Will my censure dare to profane our laws' sacred tablets? Indeed, there are sentiments which cannot remain quiet in the breast of a man who loves his country. No matter how much he might try to conceal them, they violently agitate within him, and an imperious force obliges him to disclose them. It grieves me to think that the Venezuelan government requires reform. Although many illustrious citizens think as I do, they do not all possess sufficient boldness to state their opinion publicly in favour of the adoption of new principles. This consideration has led me to be the first in introducing a subject of the greatest importance. I recognize, in doing so, my excessive audacity in pretending to give advice to the nation's highest counselors.

The more I admire the excellency of the Federal Constitution of Venezuela, the more am I convinced of the impossibility of applying it to our situation, and according to my way of thinking, it is a miracle that its model in North America has existed with so much prosperity, and not been thrown into confusion on the first appearance of danger or embarrassment. Nevertheless, the North American people are a singular example of political virtue and moral rectitude. Liberty has been its cradle, it has grown up in liberty, and it is maintained by pure liberty. I will add that that people is unique in the history of the human race, and repeat that it is a miracle that a system as weak and complicated as the federal should have existed under so difficult and delicate circumstances as those which have occurred. However, regardless of the success of this form of government in North America, the idea never even entered my head that we might compare the situation and nature of two nations so distinct as the Anglo and Spanish Americans. Would it not be extremely difficult to apply to Spain the political, civil, and religious code of Great Britain? It would be even more difficult for the laws of North America to be adopted in Venezuela. Do we not read in Montesquieu's *Spirit of the Laws* that laws should be suited to the people making them, and that it is extremely unlikely that the laws of our nation will suit another? Furthermore, we have learned that the laws ought to be related to the physical state of a country, to its climate, to the quality of its soil, to its situation and its extent and to its inhabitants' ways of life. That the laws should pay attention to the degree of liberty that the people and their constitution can support, with regards to their religion, their inclinations, their wealth or poverty, their number, their customs, their commerce and their morals.

I now present the code, which, according to my way of thinking, we ought to adopt.

The constitution of Venezuela, although founded on the most perfect principles, differed widely from the North American constitution in one essential and most important point. The Congress of Venezuela, like its North American counterpart, shares in some of the powers exercised by the executive. Ours goes further by subdividing this power and vesting it in a collective body which consequently interrupts and inconveniences the business of government whenever its members are apart. Our triumvirate lacks, therefore, unity, duration and personal responsibility. At times it does nothing, and it lacks perpetual life, real uniformity and immediate responsibility. A government which lacks continuity can hardly be said to exist. Although the powers of the president of the United States are limited by excessive restrictions, he exercises by himself alone all the functions of Authority granted him by the Constitution. There can be no doubt that his administration must be more uniform, constant, and truly proper, than that of a power divided amongst various individuals, the composition of which cannot but be monstrous.

The judicial power in Venezuela is similar to that in America, indefinite in duration, temporary and not perpetual, and it enjoys all the independence it needs.

In adopting its federal constitution, the first Congress bowed to the spirits of the different provinces rather than to the solid idea of establishing an indivisible and concentrated republic. Our legislators were influenced by the provincials, and were carried away by the dazzling appearance of North America's happiness, thinking that the blessings she enjoyed were owed exclusively to the form of government, and not to the character of the people. And in fact, the example of the United States, with its progressive prosperity, was too flattering not to have been followed. Who could resist the glorious attraction of the full and absolute enjoyment of sovereignty, independence, and liberty? Who could resist the admiration and esteem inspired by an intelligent government, which unites at the same moment public and private rights, which forms by general consent the supreme law of individuals? Who can resist the lure of a beneficent government which employs an able, active and powerful hand to direct all its efforts at all times towards social perfection, which ought to be the end of all human institutions? But no matter how beautiful this magnificent federalist system might appear, Venezuela was not prepared for so great a good immediately after shaking off her chains. Good as well as evil can be fatal when it is sudden or excessive. Our moral constitution was not yet ready to feel the benefits of a completely representative government, which is so sublime it might be better suited to a republic of saints.

Representatives of the people! You are convened to confirm or repeal, whatever may appear to you proper to be preserved, reformed, or expunged in our social compact. It is your duty to correct the work of our first legislators, and in my opinion your task should be to conceal some of the beauties contained in our political code, because not all hearts are able to admire every beauty, and not all eyes are capable of withstanding the celestial blaze of perfection. The Book of the Apostles, the doctrine of Jesus, the divine writings, sent by a gracious providence to better mankind, so sublime and so holy, would kindle an ocean of flame at Constantinople, and the whole of Asia would fiercely burn, were the book of peace to be imposed at once as the code of religion, laws, and customs.

Permit me to call Congress's attention to a matter which may be of vital importance. Let us bear in mind that our population is neither European nor North American, but are closer to a blend of Africa and America than they are to Europe, for even Spain herself is not strictly European due to its African blood, institutions and character. It is impossible to pinpoint exactly which human family we belong to. Most of the indigenous peoples have been annihilated, the European has mixed with the American and with the African, and the African has mixed with the Indian and the European. We are all children of the same mother but our fathers are strangers and differ in origin, blood, figure and form from each other. This difference creates a bond and obligation of the greatest transcendence.

All the citizens of Venezuela enjoy political equality by virtue of their constitution. Even if that equality had not been a feature of Athens, France and North America, it would still be important for us to confirm the principle in order to correct the differences that are so apparent here. Legislators! Equality must be established and practiced immediately in Venezuela as the fundamental principle of our political system. Most wise men in every society throughout history have agreed that all men are born with equal rights to the benefits of society. It has also been accepted that all men are not born with equal capacities for achievements. All ought to practice virtue but not all do so. All ought to be brave, but not all are. All ought to possess talents, but all do not. From this arises the real distinction observed amongst individuals of the most liberally established society.[2]

If the principle of political equality be generally acknowledged, not less so is that of physical and moral inequality. It would be an illusion, an absurdity, to suppose the contrary. Nature makes men unequal in genius, temperament, strength, and character. Laws correct that difference by placing the individual in society, where education, industry, arts, sciences, and virtues give a fictitious equality properly called political and social. The union of all classes in one state is eminently beneficial, and in which diversity is multiplied in proportion to the propagation of the species. By it alone have enmities been torn up by their roots, and many jealousies, follies, and prejudices avoided!

The diversity of our origins requires firm rule combined with an infinitely delicate manner in order to manage so heterogeneous a body, as its complicated composition may be dislocated, divided and dissolved by the slightest change.

The most perfect system of government is that which produces the greatest degree of happiness, of social security, and political stability.

We had reason to hope that the laws dictated by the First Congress would bring about the happiness of Venezuela. We flatter ourselves that the laws adopted here and the stability and security that they bring will render that happiness eternal.

The problem you must resolve is this. Now that we have broken our shackles and shaken off our oppressors, how can we prevent the remains of our chains from becoming weapons that would destroy our freedom? The relics of Spanish rule will continue for a long time before we can completely destroy them. Our very atmosphere is still contaminated with the germs of despotism, and neither the flames of war nor the passing of healthy laws have yet purified the air we breathe. Our hands are indeed now free, but hearts still suffer from the effects of servitude. As Homer said, when man loses his liberty, he loses half his spirit.

Venezuela's government has always been republican, it is republican, and it should always remain so. It must be based on the sovereignty of the people, the division of powers, civil liberty, the prohibition of slavery and the abolition of monarchy and privileges. We need equality in order to reform our men, our political opinions and our public customs. Now, casting our eye over the vast terrain we must still cover, let us fix our attention on the dangers we must avoid, and let history guide us on our journey.

Athens presents us with the most brilliant example of an absolute democracy, and at the same time it provides a melancholy proof of the extreme fragility of that kind of government. Even Greece's wisest legislator did not see his republic last ten years, and he suffered the humiliation of having to recognize that absolute democracy was not able to govern any kind of society, not even the most cultivated, moral and limited, because it shines only with flashes of freedom. Let us acknowledge, then, that Solon let the world see how difficult it is to govern men through laws alone.

The Republic of Sparta produced more real effects than Solon's ingenious creation, even though it seemed a chimerical invention at first. The Lycurgus legislature produced glory, virtue, morality and therefore national happiness. Even though two kings in one state were like two monsters to devour it, Sparta suffered little from its double throne, whereas Athens enjoyed the most splendid fortune with absolute sovereignty, and the free elections of magistrates frequently renewed mild, wise and enlightened laws. Pisistratus did more good for Athens than her laws, and he was a usurper and a despot. Likewise Pericles was also a usurper, and he was Athens's most useful citizen.

The Republic of Thebes existed only during the lives of Polopidas and Epaminondas, for it is men, and not principles, that form governments. However wise codes, systems, and statutes may be, they have but little influence on society; it is virtuous, patriotic, and enlightened men that constitute republics.

The Roman Constitution brought about the greatest power and fortune that any people on earth have enjoyed. There was no exact distribution of power there. Consuls, senate and people all served also as legislators, magistrates and judges. The executive power, consisting of two consuls, had the same flaw as Sparta. Yet notwithstanding this deformity, the Roman Republic did not suffer from the disastrous discord which might be expected from a leadership consisting of two individuals, both endowed with a monarch's powers. A government whose sole inclination was war and conquest was not likely to establish the happiness of the people, however. A monstrous and purely warlike government raised Rome to the highest pitch of virtue and glory, and made the whole world a Roman Empire, showing men just how much can be achieved by political virtue, and how trivial the influence of institutions can be.

Passing from ancient to modern times, we find that England and France attract the admiration of all nations and offer eloquent lessons in every aspect of government. The revolutions in those two great states have, like brilliant meteors, filled the world with light, teaching every thinking person the rights and duties of man. They have taught us the virtues and vices of governments, and how to appreciate the intrinsic value of the theories of modern philosophers and legislators. Amazingly, the luminous trajectory of this brilliant star enlightened even the apathetic Spaniards, who entered the political whirlwind and gave ephemeral proofs of liberty. But the Spaniards quickly showed that they were incapable of living under even the mildest dominion of the law, and returned after a short blaze to their original bondage.

Legislators! This is the moment to repeat Volney's eloquent words from the dedication to his *Ruins* of Palmyra. "To the emerging countries of the Spanish Indies, to the generous leaders who guide them to Freedom, may the errors and misfortunes of the Old World teach wisdom and happiness in the New." May they never forget the lessons of experience, and profit from the experience of Greece, Rome, France, England and North America. Let us learn from them the difficult science of establishing and preserving nations with proper, just, legitimate and, above all, useful laws. Let us never forget that a government's quality does not lie in its theory, form or administrative mechanism, but on how appropriate it is to the nature and character of the people it governs.

Rome and Great Britain are the nations which have most excelled amongst the ancients and moderns. Both were born to rule and be free, and both were based on solid foundations rather than brilliant models of freedom. For this reason I therefore recommend to you, representatives, the study of the British constitution, which appears to be the one destined to produce the greatest possible good to the people who adopted it. Of course perfect as it may be, I am very far indeed from proposing that we follow it like slaves. When I speak of the British constitution I refer only to its democratic features. It is fair to call it a monarchical system, which acknowledges the sovereignty of the people, the division and equilibrium of powers, civil liberty, freedom of conscience, freedom of the press, and indeed everything that is sublime in politics. A greater degree of liberty cannot be enjoyed in any kind of republic, or in any other social order. I recommend the British constitution as the best model to those who aspire to enjoy the rights of man, and to achieve a degree of political happiness compatible with our frail nature.

If we were to adopt a legislative power similar to that of the British parliament, there would be no need to change our basic laws. Like the North Americans, we have divided our national assemblies into two houses, the representatives and the senate. The first is wisely structured, as it enjoys all the appropriate powers and it is in no need of reform. The Constitution has endowed it with the origin, form and functions required for the will of the people to be lawfully and competently represented.

If the senate was hereditary rather than elected, in my view it would be the basis and the soul of the republic. In political storms the senate would both calm the government and resist popular commotion. It would be loyal to the government out of vested interest in its own preservation, so it would always oppose the people's attacks on their leaders' jurisdiction and authority. It must be confessed that most men are ignorant of their true interests, and are continually attacking them in the hands of those to whom they are committed—the individual contends against the general mass, and the general mass against authority, and it is therefore necessary that a neutral body should exist in all governments to protect the injured, and disarm the offender. This neutral body, in order that it may be such, ought neither to derive its origin from the choice of the government, not from that of the people, but in such ways that it may enjoy complete independence, neither fearing nor expecting anything from either of those sources of authority. A hereditary senate, coming from the people, would share its interests, its opinions and its spirit, and for that reason it is not to be presumed that a hereditary senate would not follow the people's interests or forget its legislative duties. The senators in Rome, and the peers in Britain, have proven themselves the finest pillars in the glorious structure of civil and political liberty.

These senators will originally be elected by congress, and their successors in the senate should be the government's highest priority. They should be educated in a school especially set aside for the future national guardians and legislators. They will be taught the arts, the sciences, and every thing that can adorn the mind of a public man; from their earliest infancy they will be acquainted with the career destined them by providence, and from their most tender years their souls will be elevated to the dignity awaiting them.

In no manner whatever would the creation of a hereditary senate be a violation of political equality; it is not a nobility I wish to establish, because that, as has been said by a celebrated republican, would be to destroy at once equality and liberty. It is an office for which candidates ought to be prepared, as a senator needs much wisdom and the right faculties to acquire knowledge.

We should not leave everything to chance, hazard and to elections. The public is easily deceived, and although it is a fact that these senators will not necessarily be born from a virtuous womb, it is true that they will come forth endowed with a most complete education. In addition, the liberators of Venezuela are entitled to hold a high rank in the Republic forever, as the Republic owes its existence to them. I do believe that posterity would observe with great regret the extinction of the illustrious names of its first benefactors. Furthermore, it is in the national interest and for national honour that Venezuela's gratitude should preserve this race of virtuous, prudent and valiant men who have liberated it. They overcame every obstacle and made the most heroic sacrifices in order to establish the Republic. If the Venezuelan people do not applaud and rejoice at the elevation of its benefactors, then they are unworthy of their freedom, and will never be free.

A hereditary senate, I repeat, will be the foundation of the legislative power, and consequently the basis of all government. Equally, it will act as a counterpoint to the government and the people, and will be an intermediate authority to cushion the arrows which those perpetual rivals will forever shoot at each other.

In all contests the interposition of a third person becomes the means of reconciliation, and thus will the senate of Venezuela be the cement of the delicate edifice so liable to violent concussions. It will be the means of calming the fury and maintaining the harmony between the limbs and the head of this political body. Nothing can corrupt a legislative body invested with the highest honours; it will be dependent on itself alone, and will fear nothing from the people and expect nothing from the government. The only objects of government should be to repress every tendency to evil and to encourage every attempt at good, and it will be deeply interested in the existence of a society with which it shares both prosperity and adversity.

It has been most justly remarked that the British House of Lords is invaluable to the nation because it forms a bulwark for the liberties of the people. I dare add that the Venezuelan senate will not only be a bulwark for liberty, but will be the core that perpetuates the Republic.

The executive power in Great Britain is invested with all the appropriate sovereign authority, but it is also circumscribed by a triple line of ditches, barriers and defensive walls. The monarch is indeed the head of the government, but his ministers and officers depend more on the laws than on his authority, because they are personally responsible, and not even royal authority can exempt them from that responsibility. The monarch is commander-in-chief of the army and navy, he makes peace and declares war, but it is parliament alone which approves the annual budget. In order to neutralize his power, the king's person is inviolable and sacred. While he keeps his head, his hands are bound. The British monarch has three formidable rivals. First, the cabinet which is responsible to the people and to the parliament. Second, the House of Lords, which protects the people's interests in representing the nobility from which it is composed. Third, the House of Commons, the organ of the British public. As the judges are responsible for the due fulfillment of the laws, they adhere strictly to them. As the administrators of public money are accountable not only for their own violations, but even for what the government may do, they guard carefully against misappropriation.

The more you examine the nature of executive power in Britain, the more you will be inclined to think it the most perfect model for monarchy, aristocracy or democracy. Let Venezuela's people or their representatives appoint a president to exercise its executive power, and we will have taken a long stride towards national happiness.

Whichever citizen is chosen to fill this post, he will be supported by the constitution. Authorized to do good, he cannot do evil. If he submits to the laws then his ministers will cooperate with him. On the contrary, should he attempt to infringe them, his ministers will leave him standing alone before the republic, and will even impeach him to the senate. Ministers are responsible for all offences that are committed, and so they are the ones who govern, and they consider their duties as personal and will take an involved and active part in his government.

Even if a president is not a man of great talents or virtues, the lack of these essential qualities may not be an impediment to satisfactory governance, because the ministries function on their own and take responsibility for the state. However exorbitant the authority of executive power in Great Britain may appear, it would not perhaps be too great in the Republic of Venezuela.

Here congress has bound both its leaders' hands and their heads. Congress has transgressed into the executives' function, contrary to Montesquieu's advice that a representative body should not take upon itself any active principle. Instead it should make laws and make sure that they are implemented. Nothing is as dangerous to a people as a weak executive, and if it has been deemed necessary to endow it with so many attributes in a monarchy, how infinitely more indispensable would it be in a republic. Let us fix our attention on this difference, and we shall find that the equilibrium of power ought to be distributed in two ways. In a republic, the executive ought to be the strongest, because everything conspires against it; and on the other hand in a monarchy the legislative ought to be the most powerful, as everything unites in favor of the sovereign. The veneration which people bear for their monarch is a proof of its prestige which works upon the superstitious respect owed to kings. The splendour of the throne, the crown and the purple; the formidable support given by the nobility, the immense riches accrued by generations of the same dynasty, and the fraternal protection offered by kings to each other, are all considerable advantages which militate in favor of royal authority, and render it almost unlimited. Those very advantages are a good reason why a republican president should be endowed with greater power than a constitutional prince.

A republican president is an individual who is isolated in the midst of society, entrusted with the duty of curbing the impetus of the people towards licentiousness, and the propensity of judges and administrators to an abuse of the laws. He is a single individual who must resist the combined attack of the opinions and interests of the legislative body, the senate and the people. He is also opposed by the passions of society, which as Carnot says, is constantly struggling between the desire to be governed and the desire not to be subject to any authority. The president is, in short, just one athlete opposed to a crowd of others. The only corrective to such weakness is for the executive power to be able to resist, vigorously and appropriately, the opposition of the legislative body and the people. If the executive does not possess the means to exercise all the authority properly placed at its disposal, it will become insignificant and the government will expire. It will leave only anarchy, usurpation and tyranny as its heirs and successors.

Let the whole system of government, therefore, be strengthened, and a system of balances established in such a way that its refinement does not lead directly to its own overthrow. No other form of government is as weak as a democracy, so its constitution must be as solid as possible, and its institutions conducive to stability. If we fail in this, we will be sure to only have a government on trial, and not a permanent system. We will inevitably have to suffer a wavering, tumultuous and anarchical community, rather than a social establishment in which happiness, peace and justice can rule.

Legislators! Let us not be presumptuous, but be moderate in our pretensions. It is by no means likely that we can do what had never yet been accomplished by any of the human rare, what the greatest and wisest nations have never effected. Undefined liberty and absolute democracy are the rocks on which republican hopes and expectations have been wrecked.

Take a look at the republics of antiquity, and those of modern times, and of those rising into existence, and you will find that almost all have been frustrated in their attempts. Men who long for legitimate institutions and social perfection undoubtedly deserve all praise. But who can say that even the wisest men practice all the virtues which the union of power and justice imperatively demand? Only angels, not men, can exist free and happy in the exercise of sovereign power.

Whilst the people of Venezuela exercise the rights they lawfully enjoy, let us moderate the excessive pretensions which an incompetent form of government might suggest. Let us give up that federal system which does not suit us. Let us renounce the triumvirate executive power, and center all executive power in the figure of a president. Let us give that president enough authority to enable him to resist the inconvenient consequences of our recent struggles, from the state of warfare we have been suffering under, and from the many foreign and domestic enemies we have had to deal with, and with whom we must contend for the time to come. Let the legislative power give up the powers which pertain to the executive, and consequently acquire fresh consistency and fresh influence in the balance of powers. Let the courts of justice be reformed by permanent and independent judges, by the introduction of juries and civil and criminal codes, not dictated by antiquity or conquering kings, but by the voice of nature, by the cry of justice and by the spirit of wisdom.

It is my anxious wish that every part of the government and administration should acquire that degree of vigour which can only sustain a due equilibrium. I desire this not just amongst the members of government, but also amongst our various social groups. A weaker political system would not matter, if it did not inevitably bring in its train the dissolution of the social body, and the ruin of all. Battlefield cries and tumultuous assemblies all appeal to heaven against the inconsiderable and blind legislators who have thought they could enjoy impunity whilst they played and experimented with our institutions. All nations on earth have sought after liberty, some by arms, and others by laws, passing alternately from anarchy to despotism, or from despotism to anarchy, but very few have been satisfied with moderate attainments, or adopted constitutions appropriate to their means, nature and circumstances.

Let us not attempt what is impossible; for if we climb too high in the regions of liberty, we will fall into the lands of tyranny. From absolute liberty there is always a descent to absolute power, and the medium between the two extremes is supreme social liberty. Abstract ideas give rise to the pernicious idea of unlimited liberty. Let us act so that the power of people is restrained within the limits pointed out by reason and interest. Let the national will be curbed by a just authority. Let civil and criminal legislation and the constitution rule imperiously over the judicial power. Then there will be balance, and we will avoid the differences and discords which would hinder questions of state, and avoid complicating matters such that we shackle rather than unite society.

A stable government needs to be based on a national spirit, which will incline everyone towards two principal points. These are moderation in public will, and limitation in public authority. It will be difficult to fix the terms of these points, but it may be supposed that the best rule for us will be reciprocal restriction and concentration. This will produce the least friction possible between legitimate will and legitimate power. This science will be learned through practice and experience. The more knowledge we have, the greater our practical skills will be. Spiritual integrity leads to knowledge and enlightenment.

Love of country, laws, and magistrates ought to be the ruling passion in the breast of every republican. Venezuelans love their country but not its laws, because these have been bad, and the source of evil. Therefore, how could they respect their leaders, as the old ones were wicked, and the new ones are hardly known? If there is no sacred respect for country, laws, and constituted authorities, then society will struggle in a state of confusion, marred by daily physical combat between men.

All our moral powers will be insufficient to save our incipient republic from such chaos unless we can unify our people, our government and our legislation in national unity. Our motto must be unity, unity, unity. Our citizens' blood is diverse: so let us mix it. Our constitution has divided authority: so let us agree to unite it. Our laws are the sad remains of all ancient and modern despotisms: so let the monstrous structure be demolished, let it fall, and withdrawing from its ruins, let us erect a temple to justice, and under the auspices of its sacred influence, let us discuss a code of Venezuelan laws. If we wish to consult records and models of legislation, then we can look to Great Britain, France, and North America.

Popular education ought to be the first care of congress's paternal regard. Morals and knowledge are the republic's cardinal points. Morals and knowledge are what we most need now.

Let us borrow from Athens her Areopagus, and her guardians of customs and laws. Let us take from Rome her censors and domestic tribunals. Let us form a holy alliance from these moral institutions. Let us renew in this world the idea of a people which is not content only to be free and powerful, but which desires also to be virtuous. Let us take from Sparta her austere establishments, and from these three springs a reservoir of virtue. Let us give our republic a fourth power with authority to preside over men's infancy and their hearts, giving them public spirit, good habits, and republican morality. Let us constitute this Areopagus to watch over the education of youth and national instruction, to purify whatever may be corrupt in the republic, to guard against ingratitude, unpatriotic feeling and idleness, and to pass judgment on the first germs of corruption and pernicious example. We should correct customs with moral punishments, just as the law punishes crime with corporal punishment. We should correct not only what may offend the laws, but what may ridicule them, not only what may attack them, but what may weaken them, and not only what may violate the constitution, but whatever may infringe on public decency.

The jurisdiction of this most sacred tribunal will encompass all education and instruction, and will only advise on penalties and punishments. Therefore its annals and records, recording its acts and its deliberations, will be the registers of virtue and vice, and will be testament to the public's moral principles and its actions. The people will consult these books when they come to vote, leaders will consult them when they choose policy, and judges will consult them for guidance in their decisions. Although such an institution might at first appear chimerical, it is in fact infinitely easier to bring about that other less useful ideas suggested by legislators of these days or of ancient times.

Legislators! When you read the constitutional project than I have respectfully submitted for your consideration, you will discover the spirit which has inspired me.

In proposing the division of our people into active and passive citizens, I have endeavoured to stimulate national prosperity by employing the two great levers of industry: labour and knowledge. Stimulated by those two powerful causes, the greatest difficulties may be overcome, and men will be made respectable and happy.

In imposing fair and prudent restrictions on the suffrage for primary and electoral assemblies, I have placed a first barrier against popular licentiousness. In this way we will avoid those injurious and tumultuous meetings which always have prejudicial consequences in elections, and for the leaders and governments chosen by them. These constraints are necessary because elections are of primordial importance in generating a people's liberty or its slavery.

In increasing the weight of congress in the balance of power, by increasing the number of legislators and by altering the senate's nature, congress is given a fixed basis making it the nation's primary body, and it is invested with great importance for the exercise of its sovereign functions.

In distinctly separating the executive from the legislative power, I do not intend to divide these supreme authorities, but rather to unite them with bonds of harmony proceeding from independence.

In investing the executive with a power and authority much exceeding what it hitherto possessed, by no means do I intend to enable a despot to tyrannize the republic. Indeed, I wish to prevent governmental despotism from bringing about a circle of despotic upheavals, in which anarchy would be alternately replaced by oligarchy and monocracy.

In soliciting the independence of judges, the establishment of juries, and a new legal code, I seek to establish the security of civil liberty. This is the most estimable, the most equitable, the most necessary, and in one word the only liberty, as without it, all others become null and void. I request the correction of the most lamentable abuses in our judicial system, which derive their origin from the filthy pit of Spanish legislation, which has collected in it the fruits of various ages, and various sources, from folly as well as talent, from good sense as well as extravagance, and from genius as well as caprice. This judicial encyclopedia has been a ten-thousand-headed monster which has up to now tortured the Hispanic nations. The affliction of Spanish legal heritage has been the fiercest calamity that heaven's anger ever permitted against that unfortunate empire.

Meditating on the most efficient mode of regenerating the character and habits which tyranny and war have given us, I have dared to suggest a moral power, drawn from the remote ages of antiquity and those obsolete laws, which for some time maintained public virtue amongst the Greeks and Romans. Although it may be considered a mere whim of fancy or even impossible, I flatter myself that you will not altogether overlook this proposal which, when honed by experience and knowledge, may prove to be very effective.

I have been horrified by the disunity which has existed among us, and which will continue to plague us while we are ruled by a federative system. I have therefore been persuaded to solicit you to adopt the centralization and union of all the states of Venezuela into a single and indivisible republic. This measure is so urgent, vital, and redeeming that without it the only fruit of our freedom would be death.

It is my duty, legislators, to present you with a detailed and accurate picture of my political, civil, and military administration, but to do so now would exhaust your valuable attention too much, and rob you of precious time at this pressing moment. My secretaries of state will therefore give an account to the congress of their various departments, and will show you at the same time the relevant documents and records which will thoroughly acquaint you with the current state of the republic.

I would not talk of the most important events of my administration if they did not directly concern the majority of Venezuela. I will draw your attention only to the most important resolutions of the most recent period of the revolution. The land of Venezuela was covered with the black veil of horrid, atrocious, and impious slavery. Our skies were filled with stormy clouds which threatened us with a fiery downpour. I implored the protection of the god of humanity, and then redemption dissipated the storms. Slavery broke its chains, and Venezuela found itself with new and grateful sons. They turned the instruments of their bondage into the weapons of their freedom. Yes! Those who were slaves are now free. Those who were the enemies of a wicked imperial stepmother are now defenders of their own country. I leave to your sovereign authority the reform or repeal of all my statutes, and decrees, but I implore you to confirm the complete emancipation of the slaves, just as I would beg for my life or for the salvation of the Republic.

The military history of Venezuela reminds us of the history of republican heroism amongst the ancients. Venezuela has made as brilliant sacrifices as any on the sacred altar of liberty. The noble hearts of our generous warriors have been filled with the most sublime and honourable feelings that have ever been attributed to the benefactors of the human race. Not fighting for power or fortune, nor even glory, but for liberty alone; the title of "Liberators of the Republic" has been their worthy recompense. I formed an association of those gallant heroes and instituted the order of liberators of Venezuela. *Legislators!* You confer honours and decorations, and you are obliged to exercise that solemn act of national gratitude.

The liberators' virtue and disinterest is proved by their having given up all their former benefits and advantages. They are men who have experienced the cruelest suffering in a most inhuman war. They have laboured under the most painful privations and the bitterest anguish. They are men who deserve the government's attention and the country's gratitude. I have therefore ordered them to be recompensed by the nation.

If I have acquired any merit in the eyes of my countrymen, I entreat you, representatives, to hear my appeal in consideration of my humble services. Let congress order a distribution of national property to the veterans of the Venezuelan army, in accordance with the law that I passed in the name of the Republic.

Now that our many victories have destroyed the Spanish armies, the court of Madrid has despairingly and vainly appealed to the magnanimous sovereigns who have just eradicated usurpation and tyranny from Europe. Those sovereigns should be the natural protectors of America's cause and its legitimacy. Spain has resorted to this insidious policy because it has been unable to reduce us to submission by force of arms. Ferdinand humbled himself so far as to confess that without that assistance of foreign aid, he could not force us back under his ignominious yoke; a yoke which no mortal power can oblige us to submit to. Venezuela is convinced that she possesses sufficient strength to repel her oppressors. Venezuela has declared through the official government channels that her fixed and final determination is to fight to the death in defence of her political life, not only against Spain, but even against the universe, should the universe be so degraded as to take the side of a government that seeks to devour us, whose only weapons are the sword of extermination and the shrieks of the Inquisition; a government that no longer seeks colonies or cities or slaves, but rather deserts, ruins and tombs. The Declaration of the Independence of the Republic of Venezuela is the most glorious, the most heroic, and the most dignified act of a free people; and it is with peculiar satisfaction that I have the honour of laying it before congress, sanctioned as it is by the unanimous approval of the free people of Venezuela.

Since the second period of the Republic, our armies have lacked the essentials of warfare. They never had enough weapons, and were at all times badly equipped. But now the defenders of independence are not only armed with justice, but also with power, and our troops may rank with the best in Europe, now that they possess equal means of destruction.

We owe these enormous advantages to the unbounded liberality of some generous foreigners who, hearing the groans of suffering humanity and seeing the cause of freedom, reason, and justice about to perish, could not remain quiet but rushed to help us with generosity and philanthropy so that our shared principles could triumph. Those friends of humanity are America's guardian angels, and to them we owe a debt of eternal gratitude, as well as a religious fulfillment of the sacred obligations we have contracted with them. The national debt, legislators, is the store of Venezuela's good faith, its honour, and its gratitude. Respect it as if it were a holy ark which contains not only the rights of our benefactors, but the glory of our loyalty. Let us perish first rather than default, in even the smallest detail, in the completion of those pledges, which have saved our country and her sons' lives.

The union of New Granada and Venezuela into one great state has been the uniform and ardent wish of the people and governments of these republics. This union, so desired by every American, has been brought about by the fortune of war, and we found ourselves effectively united already. These fraternal peoples have entrusted you with their interests, rights and destinies. In thinking of the union of this immense region, my soul soars to the stupendous height necessary for contemplating so astounding a picture. Flying from age to age, my imagination reflects on future centuries, and with admiration and amazement I see that this vast region will have acquired prosperity, splendour, and life. Swept on, I see my beloved native land in the center of the universe and watch it expand herself to the extensive coasts between those oceans, which nature has separated, and which our country will have united with large and capacious canals. I see our country as the bond, the center, and the emporium of the family of man. I see her sending the treasures of her mountains of gold and silver out to the whole world. I see her distributing her healthy plants to give life to the suffering men of the Old World. I see her imparting her inestimable secrets to the wise men in other regions who are presently ignorant of how her collective knowledge transcends even material riches. I see my country seated on the throne of freedom, wielding the sceptre of justice, and crowned with glory, displaying the majesty of the modern world for the appreciation of the ancients.

Legislators! Please look indulgently on this declaration of my political vision, on my heartfelt desires and my earnest pleas, which I have dared to address to you in the name of the people. Grant Venezuela a government which is eminently popular, eminently just, and eminently moral, which will enchain oppression, anarchy, and crime. A government for the reign of innocence, philanthropy, and peace. A government for the triumph of equality and liberty under the rule of law.

Gentlemen! You may begin your work. Mine is done.

The congress of the Republic of Venezuela is installed. In it, from this moment, national sovereignty is centred. We all owe it our obedience and loyalty. My sword, and the swords of my illustrious comrades-in-arms, will protect its solemn authority.

God save congress!

NOTES

1 The text is a revised and updated version of the original *Speech of General Bolívar to the Congress of Venezuela,* translated and published by the British merchant James Hamilton in Angostura within days of Bolívar's speech.
2 Bolívar here makes a distinction between "active" and "passive" citizens, which was uncontroversial at the time, where the former were entitled to full political rights (voting, holding offices) and the latter were entitled to be represented by the active citizens who were felt to be better qualified for those duties (whether by ethnicity/lineage, wealth or education).

REPORT ON THE BATTLE OF CARABOBO

25 June 1821

Though celebrated as a political thinker and leader, Bolívar's success as a military chief was just as important in assuring his status as the principal figure in Gran Colombian political life. Bolívar realized that political and military strategies were interlinked. His victory at the Battle of Carabobo (24 June 1821) opened the way to the definitive occupation of Caracas. This report of the victory of the republican forces shows the diversity of units under Bolívar's command.

Most Excellent Sir,

Yesterday the political birth of the Republic of Colombia was confirmed by a splendid Victory.[1]

The divisions of the liberating army having joined in the plains of Tinaquillo on the 23rd, we marched yesterday morning on the headquarters of the enemy in Carabobo.

The first division composed of the brave British battalion, the Bravo of the Apure, and 1,500 cavalry, under the orders of General Páez. The second composed of the second brigade of guards, the battalions of Tirolleurs, Boyacá and Vargas, and the sacred squadron commanded by the undaunted Colonel

Arismendi, under the orders of General Cedeño. The third composed of the first brigade of guards, the battalions of rifles, grenadiers, Vanquisher of Boyacá, Anzoategui, and the intrepid Colonel Rondón's regiment of cavalry, under the orders of Colonel Plaza.

Our march across the mountains and through the canyons, which separated us from the enemy's camp, was rapid and orderly. At eleven in the morning we marched to our left in front of the enemy, and under his fire; we crossed a stream, where only one man could pass at a time, in presence of an army placed on an inaccessible level height, commanding us in every direction.

The gallant General Páez at the head of the two battalions of his division, and the brave Coronel Muñoz's regiment of cavalry, attacked the enemy's right with such fury, that in half an hour he was thrown into confusion and completely routed. It is impossible to do sufficient honour to the valour of our troops. The British battalion commanded by the meritorious Colonel Farriar distinguished itself amongst so many other brave men, and suffered a heavy loss of officers.

The conduct of General Páez in this last and most glorious victory of Colombia renders him deserving of the highest military rank, and I therefore in the name of congress offered on the field of battle to appoint him General-in-Chief of the army.

None of the second division partook in the action except a part of the Tirolleurs of the Guard commanded by the worthy Commandant Heras. But its General, enraged that all his division could not from the obstacles of the ground join in the battle, charged singly a mass of Infantry, and felt in its centre in the heroic manner that ought to close the glorious career of the bravest of Colombia's brave. In General Cedeño the Republic has lost a staunch supporter both in war and peace and none more valiant than he, none more obedient to his government.

I recommend the ashes of the gallant hero to the sovereign congress, that the honours of a solemn triumph may be paid to his memory.

In similar grief does the Republic suffer the loss of the dauntless Colonel Plaza, who filled with an unparalleled enthusiasm threw himself on a battalion of the enemy forcing it to surrender. Colonel Plaza is deserving of Colombia's tears, and that congress confer on him the honours due to so distinguished heroism.

The enemy being dispersed, the ardor of our chiefs and officers was so great in the pursuit, that we sustained considerable loss in that high class of the army. The bulletin will communicate their illustrious names.

The Spanish army exceeded 6,000 men composed of all the best of the pacifying expeditions. That army has ceased to exist: only 400 men will have this day sought refuge in Puerto Cabello.

The Liberating army had an equal force to that of the enemy, but not more than a fifth part of it decided the fortune of the day. Our loss is not great: hardly 200 killed and wounded.

Colonel Rangel, who performed prodigious feats, as he always does, marched this day to take up positions against Puerto Cabello.

May it please the sovereign congress to accept in the name of the heroes whom I have the honour to command, the homage of a conquered army, the most numerous and the finest that ever in Colombia carried arms in a field of battle.

I have the honour to be with the highest consideration, most excellent sir, your excellency's most obedient humble servant,

Simón Bolívar
Headquarters of the Liberating Army, Valencia, 25 June 1821.
To his Excellency the President of the General Congress of Colombia.

NOTE

1 The text produced here was the first English translation of Bolívar's report, which was published simultaneously in Spanish, French and English in *El Correo del Orinoco,* 25 July 1821.   The identity of the original translator is unknown.

12

MY DELIRIUM ON CHIMBORAZO

1822

*After the great military victories of Boyacá, Carabobo and Pichincha
had expelled the Spanish army from Gran Colombia, Bolívar made his
way south to lead the wars of independence in Peru. On his way, in
Ecuador, he stopped to climb Mount Chimborazo and reflect upon his
achievements thus far.*

I was coming along, cloaked in the mantle of Iris, from the
place where the torrential Orinoco pays tribute to the god
of waters.[1] I had visited the enchanted springs of Amazonia,
straining to climb up to the watchtower of the universe. I
sought the tracks of La Condamine and Humboldt, following
them boldly. Nothing could stop me. I reached the glacial
heights, and the atmosphere took my breath away. No human
foot had ever blemished the diamond crown placed by
Eternity's hands on the sublime temples of this lofty Andean
peak. I said to myself: Iris's rainbow cloak has served as my
banner. I've carried it through the infernal regions. It has
ploughed rivers and seas and risen to the gigantic shoulders of
the Andes. The terrain had leveled off at the feet of Colombia,
and not even time could hold back freedom's march. The war
goddess Bellona has been humbled by the brilliance of Iris.
So why should I hesitate to tread on the ice-white hair of this

giant of the earth? Indeed I shall! And caught up in a spiritual tremor I had never before experienced, and which seemed to me a kind of divine frenzy, I left Humboldt's tracks behind and began to leave my own marks on the eternal crystals girding Chimborazo. I climb as if driven by this frenzy, faltering only when my head grazes the summit of the firmament. At my feet the threshold of the abyss beckons.

A feverish delirium suspends my mental faculties. I feel as if I were aflame with a strange, higher fire. It was the God of Colombia taking possession of me.

Suddenly, Time appears to me as an ancient figure weighed down by the clutter of the ages: scowling, bent over, bald, his skin lined, scythe in hand . . .

"I am the father of the centuries, the arcanum of fame and secret knowledge. My mother was Eternity. Infinity sets the limits of my empire. There is no tomb for me, because I am more powerful than Death. I behold the past, I see the future, and the present passes through my hands. Oh, child, man, ancient, hero, why such vanity? Do you think your Universe matters? That you exalt yourself merely by scaling one of the atoms of creation? Do you imagine that the instants you call centuries are enough to fathom my mysteries? Do you believe you have seen the Holy Truth? Are you mad enough to presume that your actions have value in my eyes? Compared to my brother, Infinity, everything is less than the tiniest point."

Overcome by a sacred awe, I answered: "Oh, Time, how can a wretched mortal who has climbed so high not simply vanish in thin air? I have surpassed all men in fortune, because I have risen to be the head of them all. I stand high above the earth with my feet; I grasp the eternal with my hands; I feel the infernal prisons boiling beneath my footsteps; I stand gazing at the glittering stars beside me, the infinite suns; I measure without astonishment the space that encloses all matter, and in your face I read the History of the past and the thoughts of Destiny."

"Observe," he said to me, "learn, hold in your mind what you have seen. Draw for the eyes of those like you the image of the physical Universe, the moral Universe. Do not conceal the secrets heaven has revealed to you. Tell men the truth."

The apparition disappeared.

Absorbed, frozen in time, so to speak, I lay lifeless for a long time, stretched out on that immense diamond serving as my bed. Finally, the tremendous voice of Colombia cries out to me. I come back to life, sit up, open my heavy eyelids with my own hands. I become a man again, and write down my delirium.

Simón Bolívar

NOTE

1 Bolívar's authorship of this document is sometimes doubted by historians; its overblown rhetorical and poetic style are intended to be read in a metaphorical sense to confirm Bolívar's bravery and sense of the immensity of the political goals he set himself. (For example it is unlikely that Bolívar was able to climb Chimborazo—at 6,267m above sea level—without breathing assistance). Most historians agree that if he didn't write it himself as a journal entry—no original survives—then it was probably transcribed by a close aide or friend after conversation with Bolívar in the days or weeks after the ascent. It was first published only in 1833.

13

DECREE ON CAPITAL PUNISHMENT FOR CORRUPT OFFICIALS

12 January 1824

During warfare and times of political crisis Bolívar believed that capital punishment was a fair and just public retribution against criminals who undermined social order and stability. This was as true in 1817 when Manuel Piar was executed for plotting against Bolívar's consolidated unified leadership of the Revolution, as it was in 1825 when Bolívar saw that financial stability was essential for maintaining Colombia's reputation in the eyes of the international community—particularly Britain, with whom the republic was in the process of negotiating a commercial treaty and official recognition. This text, urging its 'harsh and extreme measures,' is a typically bullish justification for the recourse to the death penalty.

Considering:

First, that one of the principal causes of the disasters in which the Republic has become embroiled was the scandalous waste of its funds by certain officials who have had access to them;

Second, that the only way to eradicate this disorder completely is to dictate harsh and extreme measures, I have decided to issue this decree at once;

Decree:

Article 1. Any public official convicted in summary court of having misapplied or stolen more than ten pesos from the public funds shall be subject to capital punishment.

Article 2. The judges assigned jurisdiction in such a case, according to law, but who fail to adhere to this decree shall be condemned to the same penalty.

Article 3. Any citizen can charge public officials with the crime specified in Article 1.

Article 4. This decree shall be posted in all the offices of the Republic and taken in account in all commissions issued to officials who are in any way involved in the handling of public funds.

It shall be printed, publicized, and circulated.

Signed into law in the Dictatorial Palace of Lima on 12 January 1824, fourth year of the Republic.

Simón Bolívar
Liberator President, etc.
Lima, 12 January 1824

By order of His Excellency, *José Sánchez Carrión*

14

DECREE ON INDIAN LABOUR

20 May 1820

At the Congress of Cúcuta in 1820 Bolívar sought to abolish the many varieties of "personal service" which had been unwillingly extracted from indigenous peoples since the Spanish conquest. In the name of citizenship and equality Bolívar sought to make a symbolic gesture which would set the independent republics apart from the colonial rule they had overthrown.

Wishing to correct the abuses practiced in Cundinamarca in most of the native villages, against their persons as well as their communal lands and their freedom, and considering that this segment of the population of the republic deserves the most paternal attention from the government because they were the most aggrieved, oppressed, and humiliated during the period of Spanish despotism, in view of the provisions of canonical and civil laws, I have decided to decree and do hereby decree:[1]

Article 1. All the lands whose titles identify them as part of the communal reserves [*resguardos*] shall be returned to the Indians as the legitimate owners, despite any legal claims alleged by the current landholders.

Article 2. The liens against these reserves, having no approval from the authority empowered to grant it, now or in the past, shall be declared null and void even if they have subsisted since time immemorial.

Article 3. Once the usurped land has been restored to the reserves, the *jueces políticos* shall allot to each family as much land as it can reasonably farm, taking into consideration the number of people that make up the family and the total extent of the reserves.[2]

Article 4. Should there be surplus acreage after the reserve lands have been parceled to the families as specified above, it shall be leased at auction by these same *jueces políticos* to the highest bidder with the best collateral, giving preference in case of equal bids to those currently in possession.

Article 5. The families, or family members, shall not be permitted to lease the allotment they own without first informing the *juez político*, so as to avoid any damage and fraud that might ensue.

Article 6. The income from the lands leased according to the provisions of Article 4 above shall be applied in part to the payment of tribute and in part to the payment of the salaries of teachers in the schools to be established in each town. Each teacher shall earn an annual salary of 120 pesos if the rental income equals or exceeds this amount; if it amounts to less, the entire sum shall be for the teacher.

Article 7. The *juez político*, in consultation with the priest of each town, shall appoint these teachers and notify the provincial governors of these appointments so that they can notify the governor of the department.

Article 8. The political governors of the provinces shall establish the regulations to be observed in the schools of their respective provinces, detailing the methods to be used in teaching and education.

Article 9. All children between the ages of four and fourteen shall attend the schools, where they shall be taught reading, writing, arithmetic, the principles of religion, and the rights and obligations of men and citizens in Colombia according to the laws.[3]

Article 10. When the money for teachers' salaries has been deducted, the remaining income from land rental shall be applied to the payment of tribute, deducting this sum from the general total owed by the town so benefited on a pro rata basis.

Article 11. In order that these operations shall be carried out with all the method, order, and precision required for the general benefit of the towns, the *jueces políticos* shall be obliged to keep a running account of the rent monies and shall present this along with the account of the tributes to the respective administrators of the public treasury.

Article 12. Neither the priests, nor the *jueces políticos*, nor any other person, employed by the government or not, shall be allowed to exploit native peoples in any manner at any time without paying them a wage previously stipulated in a formal contract witnessed and approved by the *juez político*. Anyone violating this article shall pay double the value of the service performed, and the *jueces políticos* shall exact this fine without exception in favour of the aggrieved person for any complaint, however slight; when the *jueces políticos* themselves are the violators, the political governors shall be responsible for exacting said fines.

Article 13. The same provisions of Article 12 apply to religious confraternities whose cattle shall not be pastured on reserve lands unless they pay rent, nor shall they be herded by Indians except under the terms laid down in Article 12.

Article 14. As of this moment, certain scandalous practices that are contrary to the spirit of religion, to the discipline of the church, and to all law shall be terminated without exception, including the practice of denying the sacraments to parishioners who have not paid dues for guild membership or for maintenance of the priest, as well as the practices of obliging them to pay for festivals in honour of the saints and demanding parish fees from which Indians are exempted in consideration of the stipend given to the priests by the state. Any priest found to be violating the provisions of this article by continuing these abuses shall suffer the full rigour of the law, and the *jueces políticos* shall monitor the conduct of the priests, notifying the government of the slightest infraction observed in this regard so that appropriate action can be taken.[4]

Article 15. The Indians, like all other free men in the Republic, can come and go with their passports, sell their fruit and other products, take them to the market or fair of their choice, and practice their craft and talents freely as they choose to do so and without impediment.

Article 16. Not only shall the present decree be publicized in the usual manner but the *jueces políticos* shall instruct the Indians as to its content, urging them to demand their rights even though it be against the judges themselves and to initiate action against any infraction committed.

Article 17. The vice president of Cundinamarca is charged with the observation and execution of this decree.

Issued in the General Headquarters of Rosario de Cúcuta, on 20 May 1820, tenth year of the Republic.

Simón Bolívar

NOTES

1 Although the original Spanish refers to either *naturales* or *indígenas*, the translator Frederick Fornoff prefers "Indian" in order to avoid the clumsy English term *indigene* or the confusing *native* (since Bolívar himself, for example, was a *native* of Venezuela, having been born there). Elsewhere in this volume the terms "indigenous peoples" or "indigenous communities" are used to translate *indios*, *indígenas* or *naturales*, depending on context.

2 A *juez político* was a political appointee rather than a judicial office, despite the literal translation being "Political Judge." This individual

was the local agent of the national executive (in this case, Bolívar's agents) at the municipal level.

3 This article makes plain Bolívar's belief that indigenous children should be the focus and beneficiaries of laws of this kind. He believed that culture and tradition meant that law-making could have little effect on the behavior of adults, and entrusted his hope in the education of children.

4 Here is one of Bolívar's most radical attacks on Catholic Church "abuses," which in later years he toned down considerably in an attempt to maintain ecclesiastical support for his government.

15

DECREE ON THE CIVIL RIGHTS OF INDIANS

4 July 1825

As President of Peru in 1825 Bolívar found himself charged with governing a population whose demographics were markedly different from those of Gran Colombia. He attempted to right historical wrongs by symbolically prohibiting the exploitation of indigenous peoples, though he quickly discovered, as have all subsequent Peruvian governments, that abolishing discrimination in theory is a very long way from abolishing it reality. Bolívar made the concept of equality the centrepiece of his call.

Considering:

I. That equality among all citizens is the basis of the constitution of the Republic;

II. That this equality is incompatible with the personal service that has been imposed on native peoples, and equally incompatible with the hardships they have endured due to the miserable conditions in which they live and the ill treatment they have suffered at the hands of officials, priests, local authorities, and even landowners;

III. That in the assignment of certain public works and services the Indians have been unfairly burdened;

IV. That they have been denied wages on fraudulent grounds for the work in which they have been traditionally involved, either willingly or by force, whether it be the working of mines or farm labour or crafts;

V. That one of the burdens most harmful to their existence is the payment of excessive and arbitrary fees that are commonly assessed them for the administration of the sacraments, I have decided to decree and do hereby decree:

1. That no person in the state shall demand personal service of the Peruvian Indians, either directly or indirectly, without first negotiating a free contract stipulating the wage for the work.

2. That the department prefects, intendants, governors and judges, ecclesiastical prelates, priests and their subordinates, landowners, and owners of mines and workshops are prohibited from working the Indians against their will in *faenas, séptimas, mitas, pongueajes*, and other types of domestic and common labour.

3. That when public works are ordered by the government for the general benefit of the community, this burden should not fall on Indians alone but all citizens should be drafted proportionally according to their numbers and abilities.

4. That the political authorities, through the mayors or municipalities, shall arrange for distribution of supplies, provisions, and other materials for the troops or any other purpose without burdening the Indians more than other citizens.

5. That the labour of workers in the mines, workshops, and *haciendas* should be paid in cash according to the wage specified in the contract, without forcing them to accept other forms of pay against their will and at levels below that commonly paid for such work.

6. That the scrupulous observance of the preceding article shall depend on the vigilance and zeal of the intendants, governors, and the territorial deputies for mining.
7. That the Indians shall not be forced to pay higher parochial fees than those stipulated in existing regulations or those legislated in the future.
8. That the parish priests and their assistants cannot negotiate these fees with the Indians without the mediation of the intendant or governor of the town.
9. Any neglect or omission in the observance of the preceding articles shall be cause for popular complaint and shall result in specific charges being brought before the courts.
10. The provisional secretary general is responsible for the execution and observance of this decree.

To be printed, published, and circulated.

Issued in Cuzco on 4 July 1825, the sixth and fourth years of the Republic.

Simón Bolívar
Liberator President of the Republic of Colombia, Liberator and Supreme Commander of Peru, etc.
Cuzco, 4 July 1825

By order of His Excellency, *Felipe Santiago Estenós*

16

ADDRESS TO THE CONSTITUENT CONGRESS OF BOLIVIA

25 May 1826

After the Spanish army had been expelled from Peru in 1825 Bolívar settled in Lima to write a new constitution for the new republic which was to be formed from the former colonial territory of Upper Peru, and which was to bear his name, Bolivia. This document, the Bolivian Constitution, was Bolívar's principal effort to synthesize his thoughts on how best to govern Spanish American republics. He tried to incorporate the lessons learned from experience (the failure of the patria boba, *as discussed earlier in the Cartagena Manifiesto, and the difficulties of governing Colombia since 1819). Bolívar here summarizes his Bolivian Constitution (which has not been included in this collection due to its length) and attempts to get his retaliation in first and rebut potential criticisms. He stressed that the modes of governance adopted at Angostura in 1819 and in Cúcuta in 1821 needed improving to assure stability and order in the new republics. The proposal for a Life President with the power to nominate a Vice-President who would automatically succeed him as President was particularly controversial at the time, and critics continue to use it as an example of Bolívar's "reactionary" turn in the last four years of his life.*

Legislators:

Legislators! As I present to you this draft of a constitution for Bolivia, I am overcome with embarrassment and trepidation as I know that I am unqualified to make laws.[1] When I reflect that all the wisdom of the ages has not been sufficient for the drafting of a perfect fundamental code of laws, and that the most enlightened legislator has sometimes been the direct promoter of human misery in parody of his divine mission, then what can I say of the soldier who, born among slaves and isolated in the wildest section of his country and has known only captives in chains and his comrades-in-arms, pledged to unshackle them?[2] I, a legislator? Your delusion in asking me, and my acquiescence in accepting, are perhaps equally foolish. I do not know who suffers most in this terrible dilemma—you, for the evils that may result from the laws that you have requested me to make, or I, for the ridicule to which your trust condemns me.[3]

I have summoned all my powers in order to convey to you my opinions on the manner of governing free men, in accordance with the accepted principles of civilized peoples, though the lessons of experience point only to long periods of disaster, interrupted by only the briefest intervals of success. What guides should be followed amidst the gloom of such disheartening precedents?

Legislators! Your duty compels you to avoid a struggle with two monstrous enemies, who, although they are themselves ever locked in mortal combat, will attack you at once. *Tyranny* and *anarchy* form an immense sea of oppression encircling a tiny island of freedom that is perpetually battered by the forces of the waves and the hurricane that ceaselessly threatens to submerge it. Beware, then, of the sea that you are about to cross in a fragile craft with so inexperienced a pilot at the helm.

My draft of a constitution for Bolivia provides for four branches of government, an additional one having been devised without affecting the time-honoured powers of any of the others. The electoral [legislative] branch has been accorded powers not granted it in other reputedly very liberal governments. These powers resemble, in great part, those of the federal system. I have thought it expedient and desirable, and also feasible, to accord to the most direct representatives of the people privileges that the citizens of every department, province, and canton probably desire most. Nothing is more important to a citizen than the right to elect his legislators, governors, judges, and pastors. The electoral college of each province represents its needs and interests and serves as a forum from which to denounce any infractions of the laws or abuses of the magistrates. I might, with some truth, describe this as a form of representation providing the rights enjoyed by individual governments in federal systems. In this manner, additional weight has been placed in the balance to check the executive; the government will acquire greater guarantees, a more popular character, and a greater claim to be numbered among the most democratic of governments.

Every ten citizens will elect one elector, and thus the nation will be represented by a tenth of its citizens. Ability is the only prerequisite for this post. It is not necessary to possess property to have the august right of representing popular sovereignty. The elector must, however, be able to write out his ballots, sign his name, and read the laws. He must be skilled in some trade or useful art that assures him an honest living. The only disqualifications are those of crime, idleness, and utter ignorance. Understanding and honesty, rather than wealth, are the sole requirements for exercising the public trust.

The legislative body is so composed that its parts will necessarily be in harmony. It will not find itself divided for lack of an arbiter, as is the case where there are only two chambers. Since this legislature has three parts, disagreement between two can be settled by the third. The issue is thus examined by two contending parties and decided by an impartial third party. In this way no useful law is without effect; at least it shall have been reviewed once, twice, and a third time before being discarded. In all matters between two contending parties, a third party is named to render the decision. Would it not be absurd, therefore, if in matters of the deepest concern to the nation, this expedient, dictated by practical necessity, were scorned? The chambers will thus observe toward each other the consideration which is indispensable in preserving the unity of the Congress, which must deliberate calmly and wisely and without passion. Our modern congresses, I shall be told, consist of only two houses. This is because England, which has provided the model, was forced to have the nobility and the people represented in two chambers; and, while the same pattern was followed in North America where there is no nobility, it may be presumed that the habits acquired under British rule inspired this imitation. The fact is that two deliberating bodies are always found to be in conflict. It was for this reason that Sieyès insisted on only one—a foolish classicist.

The first body [I propose] is the Chamber of Tribunes. It has the right to initiate laws pertaining to finance, peace, and war. It exercises the immediate supervision of the departments administered by the executive branch with a minimum of interference by the legislative branch.

The Senators will write the codes of law and the ecclesiastical regulations and supervise the courts and public worship. The Senate shall appoint the prefects, district judges, governors, *corregidores*, and all the lesser officials in the department of justice. It shall submit to the Chamber of Censors nominations for members of the Supreme Court, archbishops, bishops, prebendaries, and canons. Everything relating to religion and the laws comes under the jurisdiction of the Senate.

The Censors exercise a political and moral power not unlike that of the Areopagus of Athens and the censors of Rome. They are the prosecuting attorneys [*fiscales*] against the government in defense of the Constitution and popular rights, to see that these are strictly observed. Under their aegis has been placed the power of national judgment, which is to decide whether or not the administration of the executive is satisfactory.

The Censors are to safeguard morality, the sciences, the arts, education and the press. Their authority is both terrible and solemn. They are able to condemn to eternal damnation those serious criminals who usurp sovereign authority or commit other terrible crimes. They can bestow public honours upon citizens who have distinguished themselves by their probity and public service. The sceptre of glory has been placed in their hands, and so the Censors' integrity and conduct must be beyond reproach. If they stray, however slightly, they will be prosecuted. I have entrusted the preservation of our sacred rules to these high priests of the law, because it is for them to denounce whosoever profanes them.

In our Constitution the President of the Republic becomes the sun which, fixed in its orbit, radiates life to the universe. This supreme authority must be perpetual, for in non-hierarchical systems, more than in others, a fixed point is needed about which leaders and citizens, men and affairs can revolve. "Give me a point where I may stand," said an ancient sage, "and I will move the earth." For Bolivia this fixed point is the Life-Term President. Our entire order rests upon him, even though he lacks the power to act. He has been decapitated so that no one will fear his intentions, and his hands have been tied so that he can do no harm.

The President of Bolivia is endowed with many of the powers of the [North] American executive, but with restrictions that favour the people. His term of office is the same as that for the presidents of Haiti. I have chosen as Bolivia's model the executive of the most democratic republic in the world.

The island of Haiti, if you will permit this digression, found itself in a state of perpetual insurrection. Having experimented with an empire, a kingdom, and a republic, in fact every known type of government and more besides, the people were compelled to call upon the illustrious Pétion to save them. After they had put their trust in him, Haiti's destinies pursued a steady course. Pétion was made President for life, with the right to choose his successor. Thus, neither the death of that great man nor the advent of a new president imperiled that state in the slightest. Under the worthy Boyer, everything has proceeded as tranquilly as in a legitimate monarchy. There you have conclusive proof that *a life-term president, with the power to choose his successor*, is the most sublime inspiration amongst republican regimes.

The President of Bolivia will be even less dangerous than the President of Haiti because the mode of succession is better suited to serve the state's interests. Moreover the President of Bolivia is deprived of all patronage. Such restrictions on executive power have never previously been imposed in any duly constituted government. The head of the government will find that one check after another has been placed upon his authority, so that the people are ruled directly by those who exercise the most important functions in society. The priests will rule in matters of conscience, the judges in matters involving property, honour, and life, and the magistrates or men of state in all major public acts. As they owe their position, their distinction, and their fortune to the people alone, the President cannot hope to entangle them in his personal ambitions. In addition, the natural growth of opposition which any democratic government experiences throughout the course of its administration means that there is reason to believe that abuses of popular sovereignty are less likely to occur under this system than under any other.

Legislators, from this day forth liberty will be indestructible in America. Consider the wild character of our continent, whose very nature rejects monarchical rule in favor of the desert's independence. We have no great nobles or churchmen.

Our wealth has amounted to little and it is no greater today. The Church, though not without influence, does not seek domination because it is preoccupied with maintaining its position. Without these supports, tyrants cannot survive. Should any ambitious soul aspire to make himself emperor, there are Dessalines, Christophe, and Iturbide to warn him of what he may expect. No power is harder to maintain than that of a newly crowned prince. This truth, which is stronger than empires, defeated Bonaparte, the conqueror of all armies. If the great Napoleon could not maintain himself against an alliance of republicans and aristocrats, who then in America will undertake to establish monarchies upon a soil fired with the bright flames of liberty, which would consume the very pillars intended to support the royalist structure? No, Legislators, fear not the pretenders to a crown which will hang over their heads like the sword of Dionysus. New found princes who should be so bold as to erect thrones upon the ruins of liberty will instead erect tombs for their own remains, which will proclaim to future ages the fact that they *preferred vain ambition to freedom and glory*.

The constitutional limitations upon the President of Bolivia are the narrowest ever known. He can appoint only the officials of the Ministries of the Treasury, Peace, and War; and he is Commander-in-Chief of the army. These are his only powers.

Administrative functions are performed by the Cabinet, which is responsible to the Censors and subject to the close vigilance of every legislator, governor, judge and citizen. Customs officers and soldiers, who are the Cabinet's only agents, are hardly the people to win it public affection, which means that its influence will be insignificant.

There has never been a public official with as limited power as the Bolivian Vice-President. He must take orders from both the legislative and executive branches of a republican government. From the former he is given laws, and from the latter he receives commands. He must march down a narrow path between these two barriers, knowing there is a precipice on both sides. Despite these disadvantages, this form of government is better than an absolute government. Constitutional limitations increase political consciousness, thereby giving hope of ultimately finding a beacon of light which will act as a guide through the ever-present shoals and reefs. These limitations serve as dikes against the violence of our passions, which are prompted by selfish interests.

In the government of the United States it has of late become the practice for the Secretary of State to succeed the President. Nothing could be more expedient, in any republic, than this practice. It has the advantage of placing at the head of the administration a man experienced in the management of a nation. In entering upon his duties, he is fully prepared and brings with him the advantages of popularity and practical experience. I have borrowed this practice [of succession] and embodied it in the law.

The President of the Republic will appoint the Vice-President, who will administer the affairs of the state and succeed the President in office. By means of this device we shall avoid elections, which result in that great scourge of republics—anarchy, which is the handmaiden of tyranny, the most immediate and terrible peril of popular government. Compare the tremendous crises in republics when a change of rulers takes place with the equivalent situation in legitimate monarchies.

The Vice-President should be the purest of men. This is because, if the President does not appoint the most honourable of citizens, he will inevitably fear him as an ambitious and terrible enemy, and always be suspicious of his motives. The Vice-President will have to exert himself and serve faithfully in order to win the high esteem that will make him worthy of the supreme command. The people and the legislative body will expect both ability and integrity of this high ranking office, as well as blind obedience to the principles of freedom.

If hereditary succession perpetuates the monarchical system, and is all but universal, is not this plan much better, where the Vice-President succeeds to the presidency? What if hereditary princes were chosen by merit and not by fate? What if, instead of wallowing in idleness and ignorance, they were put in charge of government administration? They would unquestionably be more enlightened monarchs, and they would contribute to the happiness of their peoples. Indeed, Legislators, monarchy has won its support across the world because of the hereditary principle, which renders it stable, and by unity, which makes it strong. A monarch is brought up as a spoiled child, cloistered in his palace, reared on adulation and swayed by every passion. But, what irony, he is able to maintain order and command the subordination of his citizens, by virtue of power firmly and constantly applied. Remember, Legislators, that these advantages are also combined in the Life-President and Hereditary Vice-President that I propose.

The Judicial Power that I propose enjoys an absolute independence not to be found in any other nation. The people nominate the candidates, and the legislature chooses the individuals who will serve in the courts. The judiciary is therefore able to fulfill its obligation to safeguard individual rights, as their own power emanates from the people. These rights, Legislators, are those that ensure freedom, equality, and security—all guarantees of the social order. The real foundation of liberty resides in the civil and criminal codes, and the worst kind of tyranny is that which is exercised by the courts through that powerful instrument, law. As a rule, the executive is the custodian of public affairs, but the courts are the arbiters of private affairs—of the concerns of individuals. The judicial power determines the happiness or the unhappiness of the citizens. If the Republic enjoys justice and liberty, this can only be because of the effective operations of the Judiciary. At times, political structure is of minor importance if civil organization is perfect, which is to say, if the laws are rigorously enforced and held to be as inexorable as fate.

The use of torture and forced confessions is prohibited in keeping with the ideas of our time, as should be expected. We also shorten the procedures which allow an intricate maze of appeals to lengthen lawsuits.

The territory of the Republic will be governed by prefects, governors, *corregidores*, justices of the peace, and *alcaldes*. I have been unable to elaborate upon the internal organization and the exact authority of each of these positions. It is my duty, nevertheless, to commend to the Congress rules and regulations governing the administration of departments and provinces. Bear in mind, Legislators, that nations are composed of cities and towns, and that the happiness of a nation stems from their well-being. You can never give too much attention to the proper administration of the provinces. This is the crux of the legislative art, yet it is neglected only too often.

I have divided the armed forces into four parts: regular army, fleet, national militia, and internal revenue patrol. The duty of the army is to protect the border. God grant that it will never have to turn its weapons upon our citizens! The national militia will suffice to preserve order at home. Bolivia has no extensive coastline and therefore has no need of a navy, although the day may come when we will have both. The internal revenue patrol is in every way preferable to a civilian guard, which is not merely superfluous but evil. Accordingly, the Republic must garrison her borders with regular troops, using the revenue patrol to combat fraud at home.

I have felt that the Constitution of Bolivia may have to be amended at intervals, in accordance with the demands of changing world conditions. The amendment procedure has been provided for in terms that I consider best adapted to the subject.

The responsibility of government officials is set forth in the Bolivian Constitution in the most explicit terms. Without responsibility and restraint, the nation becomes a chaos. I should like most forcefully to urge upon you, the legislators, the introduction of strict and well-defined laws on this important matter. Everyone speaks of responsibility whilst paying it no more than lip service. When there is no responsibility, Legislators, the judges and all the other officials, high and low, abuse their powers, as there is no rigid check on government servants. The citizens, consequently, are the victims of this abuse. I recommend a law that will provide for an annual check on every government employee.

The most perfect guarantees have been provided for the individual. *Civil liberty* is the one true freedom; the others are nominal, or they affect the citizens slightly. The inviolability of the individual—the true purpose of society and the source of all other safeguards—is guaranteed. *Property rights* will be covered by a civil code, which you should wisely draft in due time for the good of your fellow citizens. I have left intact that law of laws—*equality*. Neglect it, and all rights and safeguards will vanish. We must make every sacrifice for it and, at its feet, cast the dishonoured and infamous relics of slavery.

Legislators, slavery is the negation of all law, and any law which should perpetuate it would be a sacrilege. What justification can there be for its perpetuation? Examine this crime from every aspect and tell me if there is a single Bolivian so depraved as to wish to sanctify by law this shameless violation of human dignity. One man owned by another! A man reduced to a chattel! An image of God coupled to the yoke like a beast! Where are the legal claims of the enslavers of men? Guinea did not authorize them, for Africa, devastated by fratricidal struggles, spawned nothing but crime. Now that the remnants of those African tribes have been transplanted here, what law or power has jurisdiction to sanction these victims' becoming the slaves of masters? To transmit, to ignore, to perpetuate this criminal breeder of torture would be a most detestable outrage. To establish a principle of ownership based upon a heinous dereliction cannot be conceived unless the very elements of law and rights are distorted and all our concepts of men's obligations perverted beyond recognition. No one can violate the sacred doctrine of *equality*. And can slavery exist where equality reigns supreme? Such contradictions impugn our sense of reason even more than our sense of justice. This would win us the reputation of madmen, rather than tyrants.

If there were no divine Protector of innocence and freedom, I should prefer the life of a great-hearted lion, lording it in the wilderness and the forests, to that of a captive in the keep of an infamous tyrant, a party to his crimes, provoking the wrath of Heaven. But no! God has willed freedom to man, who protects it in order to exercise the divine faculty of *free will*.

Legislators, I shall mention now one item which my conscience has compelled me to omit from the Constitution. A political constitution should not prescribe any particular religion because, according to the best doctrines, fundamental laws are to guarantee political and civil rights. Since religion has no bearing on these rights, it is by nature unrelated to public society, as its place is in the moral and intellectual sphere. Religion governs man in his home, within his own walls, within himself. Religion alone is entitled to examine a man's innermost conscience. Laws, on the contrary, deal with surface things; they are applicable outside the home of a citizen. If we apply these criteria, how can a state rule the conscience of its subjects, enforce the observance of religious laws, and mete out rewards and punishments, when the tribunals are in Heaven and God is the judge? Only the Inquisition could presume to do their work on earth. Would you bring back the incendiary ideas of the Inquisition?

Religion is the law of conscience. Any law that imposes a religion negates man's conscience, because to compel a conscience is to destroy the value of faith, which is the very essence of religion. The sacred precepts and doctrines are useful, enlightening and spiritually nourishing. We should all avow them, but the obligation is moral rather than political.

On the other hand, what are the religious rights of man on earth? These rights reside in Heaven where there is a tribunal that rewards merit and dispenses justice according to the code laid down by the great Lawgiver. As all this is within divine jurisdiction, it would seem to me, at first sight, to be sacrilegious and profane for us to interfere with the Commandments of the Lord by enactments of our own. Prescribing religion is therefore not the task of the legislator, who, for any infractions, must provide penalties, not mere exhortations. Where there are no temporal punishments or judges to apply them, the law ceases to be law.

The moral development of man should be the legislator's first concern. Once this has been achieved, man can then base his morality upon the truths revealed to him. He will acknowledge religion *de facto* and all the more effectively for having reached it through personal experience. Moreover, parents cannot neglect their religious obligations to their children. Spiritual pastors are obliged to teach the Gospel of Heaven. The example of Jesus's true disciples must be the most eloquent education in divine doctrine. But doctrine can not be commanded, and he who gives orders is no teacher. Force can play no part in the provision of spiritual counsel. God and his ministers are the only religious authorities, and religion exerts its influence solely through spiritual means and bodies. The nation's body politic is not an instrument for religion, as it serves only to direct public energies toward purely temporal ends.

Legislators, as you now proclaim the existence of the new Bolivian Nation, you must be inspired by noble, generous and elevated thoughts! The admission of a new state into world society gives humankind a cause for great celebration because it expands the great family of peoples. What a joy it is then for its founders! And a joy for me, also, upon seeing myself compared with the most celebrated of the Ancients, the founder of the Eternal City. This honour rightly belongs to the creators of nations, who as their very first benefactors truly deserve the rewards of immortality. Similarly the honour you give me is immortal, and in addition it is gratuitous because it is undeserved. Where is the Republic, where is the city that I have founded? Your magnanimity in giving my name to a nation has far outdone any services I may have rendered, for it is infinitely superior to the service of any one man.

My embarrassment increases as I contemplate the magnitude of your reward, for even if I had contributed the talents and virtues, indeed the genius, of the greatest heroes, I should still be unworthy to give the name you have desired to take— my own! Shall I express gratitude, when gratitude alone can never express, however feebly, the emotion stirred within me by your kindness, which, like that of God himself, is infinite! Yes! God alone had sovereign power to call this land Bolivia. And what does Bolivia signify? A boundless love of liberty, and, after you had received it, you, in your enthusiasm, could conceive of nothing equal to it in value. When, carried away by the immensity of your joy, you could find no adequate way to express the sweep of your emotions, you put your own name aside and adopted mine for all time to come. This act, which is without parallel in all history, is especially so in view of the sublime disinterestedness which inspired it. Your deed shall demonstrate to the ages that as yet exist only in the infinite years of the future how strongly you cherished your right—the right to exercise political virtue, to acquire sublime talents, and to know the satisfaction of being men. Your deed, I repeat, shall prove that you were indeed fit to receive that great heavenly benediction—*the Sovereignty of the People*—the sole legitimate authority of any nation.

Legislators, happy are you who preside over the destinies of a republic that at birth was crowned with the laurels of Ayacucho, a republic destined for enduring life under benign laws which, in the calm that has followed the fearful tempest of war, shall be dictated by your wisdom.

Simón Bolívar
Lima, 25 May 1826

NOTES

1 This translation is a substantially revised version of Lewis Bertrand's original.
2 The Address was first published in 1826 as *Proyecto de Constitución para la República de Bolivia y discurso del Libertador,* and in English translation in 1827.
3 There is a detailed analysis of the contradictions inherent in the text in Matthew Brown, "Enlightened Reform after Independence: Simón Bolívar's Bolivian Constitution," in Gabriel Paquette, ed., *Enlightened Reform in Southern Europe and its Atlantic Colonies, c. 1750–1830* (Aldershot: Ashgate, 2009). News of Bolívar's proposals triggered rebellions (both pro and contra) across Colombia.

17

LETTER TO JOSÉ ANTONIO PÁEZ

6 March 1826

This is a more succinct version of the previous document, the "Address to the Constituent Congress," which uses much plainer language than the Address reproduced above. Bolívar did not think highly of Páez's literacy but was also desperate for his support for the Constitution. He therefore made every effort to describe his ideas in the most accessible and persuasive terms. It provides a useful complement to the Address itself and gives a good insight into Bolívar's attempts at political relationship-building.

My dear General and friend:[1]

I have received your very important letter of October 1 last, brought to me by Guzmán, whom I have met and heard with some surprise, for his mission is truly an extraordinary one.[2] You tell me that Colombia is in a position similar to that of France when Napoleon was in Egypt, and that I, like him, should exclaim: "The plotters are wrecking the country; we must fly to her rescue." To be sure, virtually the whole of your letter is penned with the sharp point of truth, but the truth is not enough to make a plan effective. It seems to me that you have not judged the men and the events with sufficient impartiality. Colombia is not France, nor am I Napoleon. In France they think deeply, and their wisdom is deeper still. The population is homogeneous, and war had brought her to the brink of the precipice. No republic was as great as France, which throughout history had always been a kingdom. The republican government, discredited, had become the object of nearly universal execration. The monsters who ruled France were both cruel and incompetent. Napoleon was great and unique but highly ambitious. Here we have none of this. I am not, nor do I care to be, a Napoleon. I regard these examples as unworthy of the glory that I have achieved. The title of Liberator is superior to any that human pride has ever sought. It cannot, therefore, be degraded. Moreover, our people have nothing, nothing whatever, in common with the French. Our Republic has raised the country to heights of glory and prosperity, endowing it with laws and freedom. No Colombian leader is a Robespierre or a Marat.[3] The danger was over when hope began to appear; accordingly, nothing justifies the course that you propose. Republics surround Colombia on all sides, and Colombia has never been a kingdom. By its elevation as by its splendour, a throne would inspire terror. Equality would end, and the men of colour would see all their rights stripped away by a new aristocracy. In brief, my friend, I cannot see the wisdom of the plan Guzmán placed before me. I believe, moreover, that those who promoted it are the same type of men who supported Napoleon and Iturbide in order to revel in their leaders' prosperity only to abandon them in their hour of peril. If, however, those men are acting in good faith, you may be sure that they are hotheads or extremists, whatever their principles.

I shall tell you quite frankly that the plan will not benefit you, me, or the country. I believe, nevertheless, that in the next period in which the Constitution can be revised, appropriate amendments favouring sound conservative principles can be introduced without violating any republican doctrines. I shall send you a plan of a constitution that I have devised for the Republic of Bolivia, embodying full guarantees of permanency and freedom, equality and order. If you and your friends should approve this plan it would be highly desirable if you will comment upon it publicly and commend it to the people. We would thus render a service to our country—a service that will win the support of all parties except the extremists; in other words, of all those who seek genuine freedom joined with true stability. On the other hand, I would not advise you to do for yourself what I would not permit to be done for me. But if the people should express their choice by giving you the nation's vote, I should most gladly employ my sword and my authority in sustaining and defending the sovereign will of the people. This assurance I give you with the same sincerity with which I remain your constant friend.

Simón Bolívar
Magdalena, 6 March 1826

NOTES

1 Translation by Lewis Bertrand with minor amendments to update some terminology.
2 Bolívar's attempt to persuade Páez of the Constitution's merits was a failure. Páez was unimpressed and began to move towards advocating Venezuela's secession from Gran Colombia. The Cosiata Rebellion of April–September 1826 was partially triggered by unfavorable propaganda regarding the Bolivian Constitution. During *La Cosiata* Páez defied Bolívar's authority and Bolívar had to compromise and mollify him in order to avoid the disintegration of Colombia.
3 This letter shows clearly Bolívar's opinion that Gran Colombian politics operated in entirely different ways to French politics. At this time, and for much of the nineteenth century, the French example was the touchstone for Hispanic American elites, like Bolívar, who wanted their countries to become "modern," "civilized" and "prosperous." But the letter also shows that Bolívar was not uncritical; he strives to show that he is "not Napoleon" and it is Colombians, not the French, who come out favourably from the comparison with Robespierre and Marat.

18

LETTER TO JOSÉ JOAQUÍN OLMEDO

27 June 1825

In the following two letters to José Joaquín Olmedo, Bolívar shows himself to be a witty and modest literary critic. He is writing about the epic poem "Victoria de Junín," written by the Ecuadorian Olmedo in praise of the feats of Bolívar's own armies. Olmedo had been named by Bolívar as the Peruvian agent in London, and instructed him to raise a large foreign loan to support the new republic in its first years. The hyperbolic tone of Bolívar's comments here are in keeping with Olmedo's poetry. The lengthy digressions are interspersed with brief asides which are comical in their straightforwardness (i.e. "Stanza 360 seems a bit prosaic").

Dear friend:

A few days ago, while on the road, I received from you two letters and a poem.[1] The letters are those of a statesman and a poet, but the poem is that of an Apollo. The heat of the torrid zone, the fires of Junín and Ayacucho, the rays of the father of Manco Capac, never have these stirred a flame so intense in the mind of any mortal. You fly high . . . higher than any shot that was ever fired. You sear the earth with sparks from the wheel and axle of an Achilles' chariot, such as Junín never knew. You evoke characters of your own creation: of me you make a Jupiter, of Sucre a Mars, of La Mar an Agamemnon and a Menelaus, of Córdova an Achilles, of Necochea a Patroclus and an Ajax, of Miller a Diomedes, and of Lara a Ulysses. You give to each of us a divine and heroic haze that covers us like the protecting wings of a guardian angel. You mold us in your poetic and fanciful manner; and, to project the fiction of the fable into the land of poesy, you elevate us to a false deity, after the manner of Jupiter's eagle which bore the tortoise to the skies only to let it fall upon a rock, crushing it and dismembering its body. Indeed, you have raised us to such heights that you have cast us into the abyss of nothingness, eclipsing in an immensity of brilliance the pallid splendour of our dim virtues. Thus, my friend, you have pulverized us with the bolts of your Jupiter, with the sword of your Mars, with the sceptre of your Agamemnon, with the lance of your Achilles, and with the wisdom of your Ulysses. Were I less charitable or were you a lesser poet, I might choose to believe that you had intended to use the heroes of our poor comedy in order to make a parody of the *Iliad*. But no, that I do not believe. You are a poet and you fully comprehend, as did Bonaparte, that from the heroic to the ridiculous it is but a step, and that Manolo and the Cid, though sons of different fathers, are blood brothers. To an American your poem will read like a canto of Homer; to a Spaniard, like a canto from the *Facistol* of Boileau.

I thank you for it with infinite gratitude.

I am sure that you will worthily perform your mission to England. Indeed, so confident am I that, after scanning all the Empire of the Sun, I could find no diplomat more capable of representing Peru and of negotiating for her to better advantage. You are to be accompanied by a mathematician, lest you should avail yourself of poetic license and choose to believe that two and two are four thousand. Therefore, our Euclid goes along to open the eyes of our Homer, to make certain that he sees not with his imagination but with his eyes, and that he is not entranced with harmonics and metres but keeps his ears attuned only to the rude, harsh, and rasping prose of public figures and politicians.

Yesterday I came to the classic Land of the Sun, of the Incas, of fable, and of history. Here gold is the true sun. The Incas are his viceroys or prefects; fable is the story of Garcilaso [de la Vega]; history is Las Casas's account of the destruction of the Indians. But poetry aside, your every word evokes exalted ideas and profound thoughts within me. My soul is enthralled by the presence of Nature unfolding herself, creating from her own elements a model drawn from the image of her innermost inspirations, with no need of other works or counsel to guide her; nor is she influenced by the whims of humanity or contaminated by the chronicles of the crimes and follies of our species. Manco Capac, the Adam of the Indians, left his Titicacan paradise to found a historic society, unmixed with fable, either sacred or profane.

God made him into a man, and he created a kingdom. History speaks truthfully, for stone monuments, wide and straight roads, simple customs, and authentic traditions bear witness to a social organization of which we have no conception, no prototype, no imitation anywhere else. Peru is unique in the annals of man. This is how it appears to me now that I am here, and all that I have just told you, in more or less poetic vein, seems perfectly obvious.

Be so kind as to show this letter to Paredes, and, as for yourself, kindly accept the sincere assurances of my friendship.

Simón Bolívar
Cuzco, 27 June 1825

NOTE

1 This letter was first published in 1870 from the personal archive of Olmedo's father-in-law, Martín Icaza. Olmedo had gone on to be an important political figure in Guayaquil in his own right, and served as Ecuadorian President in 1845.

19

LETTER TO JOSÉ JOAQUÍN OLMEDO

12 July 1825

My dear friend:

The day before yesterday I received your letter of 15 May which I can only term extraordinary, for, without my knowledge and without asking my consent, you have taken the liberty of making a poet out of me. As every poet is obstinate, you have persisted in imputing to me your tastes and talents. Since you have paid your money and taken your choice, I shall do as did the peasant in the play, who, on being made king, said: "Now that I am King, I shall dispense justice." You must not complain, therefore, of my judgments, for, as I am not trained for the office, I shall blindly imitate the King in the comedy who sent to prison everyone he could lay his hands on. But now to our subject.

I have heard it said that one Horace wrote a very sharp letter to the Pisos in which he harshly criticized metrical compositions. His imitator, M. Boileau, has taught me a few precepts whereby a less informed man can cut to pieces anyone who speaks very prudently in a melodic and rhythmic tone.

I shall start by violating the rules of rhetoric, as I do not like to begin by praising only to end by criticizing. I shall leave my panegyrics for the end of this effort where, in my opinion, they properly belong. You should prepare yourself to hear profound truths, or rather prosaic truths, for you of course know that a poet measures truth by standards that differ from those that guide us men of prose. I shall only follow my masters.

You should have stricken out many verses that I find dull and commonplace. Either I have no ear for music, or they are—they are mere oratory. Forgive my boldness, but as you have dedicated this poem to me I can do with it as I see fit.

Next, you should have allowed your ode to stand in order to ferment like wine; it could then be drawn cold, and sipped and savoured. Haste is a grievous sin in a poet. Racine would have devoted two years to the composing of fewer verses, for which reason he is the purest versifier of modern times. The plan of your poem, though essentially good, has a capital defect in its design.

You have prepared too small a frame in which to place a giant who takes up the whole picture and whose very shadow blots out the other characters. The Inca Huayna-Capac appears to be the theme of the poem: his is the genius and gist of it: he, in brief, is its hero. On the other hand, it hardly seems proper for him to praise indirectly the religion that destroyed him, and it appears even less proper that he does not desire the reestablishment of his throne, but, instead, gives preference to foreign intruders who, although they are the avengers of his blood, are nonetheless the descendants of the destroyers of his empire. Such disinterestedness is not human. Nature must govern all rules of behaviour, and this is contrary to Nature. You will also permit me to observe that this Inca spirit, who should be lighter than air since he comes from Heaven, has too much to say and his part is too involved; that is why the poets have never forgiven *le bon Henri* for his harangue against Queen Isabelle. Hence, you see that, although Voltaire had some claim to indulgence, even he did not escape criticism.

The introduction to the ode is bombastic. It is a thunderbolt of Jupiter that splits the earth and deafens the Andes, which must bear it without a performance like that of Junín. In praising the modesty with which Homer begins his divine *Iliad*, Boileau gave us a precept: He promises little and does much. *Los valles y la sierra proclaman a la tierra*—its onomatopoeia is without appeal. And *los soldados proclaman al general*. Indeed, are the valleys and the mountains the most humble servants of the earth?

Line 360 has overtones of prose—I may be mistaken, but, if I am, why did you make me King?

Let us, to avoid dispute, cite for example line 720:

Que al Magdalena y al Rimac bullicioso . . .

And this other, 750:

Del triunfo que prepara glorioso . . ..

And there are others that I refrain from quoting in order not to appear too harsh and ungrateful toward my poet laureate.

"The tower of St. Paul becomes your Pindo, and the mighty Thames becomes the Helicon." Here your ode grows dull, and, if you will consult the shades of Milton, you can deftly apply his demons to us. There are other eminent poets from whom you could derive greater inspiration than that to be found in the Inca [Huayna-Capac], who in truth could sing nothing but the *yaravís*. Pope, the poet of your school, could teach you how to avoid pitfalls that Homer himself could not escape. You will pardon me for taking refuge in Horace as I pronounce my oracles. That critic was indignant that the author of the *Iliad* had ever nodded, and you well know that Virgil regretted having brought forth so divine a daughter as the *Aeneid* even after she had been some nine or ten years in the making. Thus, my friend, you must file and file again to polish up the works of man. I have struck land; hence, I end my critique, or, rather, my blind efforts.

I humbly confess to you that I find the versification of your poem sublime. A spirit seems to have borne you to celestial heights. Throughout most of the ode you preserve a life-giving, refreshing warmth. Some of the inspired passages are highly original. The thoughts are noble and high-minded. Your hero's lending of a bolt to Sucre is superior to Achilles' giving of his arms to Patroclus. Line 130 is most beautiful: "I hear the whirlwinds rage and see the sparks fly"—it is truly Hellenic, Homeric. In the portrayal of Bolívar at Junín we see, as in profile, the moment that precedes the combat between Turnus and Aeneas. The role you give Sucre is warlike and grand. And when you speak of La Mar you remind me of Homer singing of his friend Mentor; though the characters differ, the case is similar—but then, is not La Mar a Mentor in arms?

Permit me to ask, dear friend, where you found the inspiration with which to create an ode so well sustained from the beginning to the end? In the end the battle brings victory, and it is you who have won the battle because you close your poem with dulcet verses, elevated thoughts, and philosophic concepts. You return to the Pindaric vein, and it is so much to my liking that I would call it divine.

Pursue, my beloved poet, the happy course upon which the Muses have launched you with your translation of Pope and your *Ode to Bolívar*.

Pardon, pardon, my friend, but you are to blame for calling me a poet.

Your devoted friend,

Simón Bolívar
Cuzco, 12 July 1825

20

MEASURES FOR ECOLOGICAL PROTECTION

31 July 1829

During Bolívar's last years in power, he was preoccupied with suppressing internal and regional revolts against his rule and seldom had time for the cogent analyses of the bigger picture that had so distinguished him over his peers in previous years. There are some exceptions—this text is one. It seeks to formalize state control over Colombia's forests to harness plants for medicinal benefits as well as to control logging. Bolívar wanted to ensure that if anyone was to profit from the exploitation of the forests it should be the state, and not unscrupulous private companies or individuals.

Considering:

First, that the Forests of Colombia, those owned publicly as well as privately, represent an enormous treasure in wood suitable for all types of construction as well as dyes, quinine, and other useful substances for medicine and the arts.

Second, that throughout the region we are experiencing excessive harvesting of wood, dyes, quinine, and other substances, especially in the forests belonging to the state, with disastrous consequences.

Third, that to avoid these, it is necessary to establish regulations for the effective protection of public and private property against violations of every kind, having seen the reports compiled for the government on this matter and heard the report of the Council of State,

I hereby decree:

Article 1. The governors of the provinces shall designate in each canton, through elected judges or other trustworthy persons, common lands belonging to the Republic, specifying in writing their boundaries and botanical properties, such as precious woods, medicinal plants, and other useful substances, ordering this information to be recorded in the public archives with another copy forwarded to the prefecture.

Article 2. They shall immediately make it known in each canton that no one can harvest precious wood or timber for the construction of commercial boats from vacant or state lands without prior written permission from the governor of the respective province.

Article 3. These permits shall never be issued free of charge, but shall be subject to a graduated fee to be determined by the governor in consultation with experts who shall submit a regulation to this effect for the approval of the prefecture.

Article 4. Anyone who harvests quinine, precious wood, and timber for construction from the state forests without the proper permit, or who harvests more than the amount specified in the permit, shall incur a fine of from 25 to 100 pesos, which shall be applied to the public funds, and shall, further, reimburse the cost of harvested or damaged property, based on the assessment of experts.

Article 5. The prefects of the maritime departments shall take special care to conserve the timber in the state forests, especially that which can be used for the naval forces, and to ensure that only the specified amount is harvested, or that which will bring a profit to the public revenues.

Article 6. The governors of the provinces shall prescribe regulations that are simple and accommodated to the local circumstances so that the harvesting of wood, quinine, or plants for dyes is conducted in an orderly fashion that will improve the quality of the forests and promote greater commercial profits.

Article 7. Wherever quinine or other substances useful as medicines are present, a supervisory *junta* shall be established to oversee an area considered appropriate by the respective prefect; this *junta* shall be composed of at least three persons and, whenever possible, one of them shall be a medical doctor. The members of the *junta* shall be appointed by the prefect, on nomination by the respective governor, and they shall serve in this capacity as long as their conduct warrants.

Article 8. Anyone who intends to harvest quinine and other substances useful as medicines from forests owned by the state or by individuals shall be inspected in their operations by one or two commissioners appointed by the supervisory *junta*, salaries or expenses to be paid by the entrepreneur or entrepreneurs. The *junta* and the commissioners shall ensure:

First, that the limits specified in the permit to harvest quinine and to extract other substances useful as medicines shall not be exceeded.

Second, that the extraction and other preparations shall be done according to the regulations drawn up by the faculties of medicine in Caracas, Bogotá, and Quito, in a simple guidebook they are to compile that will have as its object the prevention of the destruction of the plants that produce these substances, which moreover are to be handled with all essential care in their preparation, bottling, etc., so that their price and commercial value will be maximized.

Article 9. In ports where no supervisory *junta* has been established, the inspection stipulated in Article 8 shall be carried out by intelligent persons appointed to this task by the governor, their report rigorously expressing the quality of the quinine or substance that has been examined. Should this requirement not be satisfied with the appropriate rigour, customs will not issue a stamp to register said substance, and should it be discovered that extraneous bark or substances lacking the necessary beneficial properties have been mixed with it, this shall be noted, the governor or customs administrator being so informed in order that shipment can be blocked.

Article 10. The faculties of medicine of Caracas, Bogotá, and Quito and the department prefects shall each provide the government with a report proposing measures to improve the extraction, preparation, and sale of quinine and other substances available for harvest in the forests of Colombia for medicinal use or for the arts, making all necessary recommendations for the increase of this important aspect of the public wealth.

The secretary of state in the Office of the Interior is charged with the execution of this decree.

Simón Bolívar
Liberator President of the Republic of Colombia, etc.
Guayaquil, 31 July 1829

For His Excellency the Liberator President of the Republic, the Secretary General, *José D. Espinar*

Part III

INTERNATIONALIZING THE REVOLUTION

21

TO THE BRAVE SOLDIERS OF THE IRISH LEGION

1 January 1820

Bolívar lent great support to the efforts of Venezuelan agents to recruit foreign mercenaries in Great Britain and Ireland. In total, around 7,000 of these adventurers reached Venezuela, though no more than 2,000 played any meaningful role in the independence wars. Most either deserted or died of disease in their first months in the New World. In 1819, however, there were still great hopes that the foreign mercenaries would lead the rebel armies to victory over Spain. Bolívar regarded them as propaganda material as much as useful soldiers or officers—upon arrival very few of the "brave soldiers of the Irish Legion" understood any Spanish, and therefore this speech was simultaneously translated so that they could comprehend the praise that Bolívar heaped upon them.

Irishmen! You have been torn from your country because you have chosen to follow the generous feelings which have always distinguished you amongst the most illustrious Europeans. I have the honour to count on you as Venezuela's adoptive sons, and as the Defenders of Colombia's Freedom.[1]

Irishmen! Your sacrifices are beyond any prize we could give you, and Venezuela does not have sufficient resources to pay you as much as you deserve. But everything Venezuela has, everything that it can dispose of, it will happily give it to the brilliant foreigners who come to give their lives to our nascent Republic. The Government and People of Venezuela will religiously fulfil the promises that have been made to you by the virtuous and brave General Devereux, in recompense for your incorporation into the Liberating Army.[2]

You can be sure that we would first prefer to give up all of our resources rather than to deprive you of your sacred rights.

Irishmen! You will find that the most just and most sublime reward is being prepared for you by History, and by the Blessings of the Modern World.

Governmental Palace, Angostura, 14 December 1819, 9o.[3]

NOTES

1 The original Spanish version was first published in *Correo del Orinoco,* 1 January 1820, and is reproduced in Matthew Brown and Martín Alonso Roa Celis, eds., *Militares extranjeros en la independencia de Colombia: Nuevas perspectivas* (Bogotá: Museo Nacional de Colombia, 2005), p.65. On the Irish Legion, see Matthew Brown, *Adventuring through Spanish Colonies,* chapters 1 and 5. Venezuela was one of the three constituent parts of the Republic of Colombia, which Bolívar had recently inaugurated (see Angostura Address, above). The other two were New Granada and Ecuador.
2 General John Devereux (1778–1860) was the leader of the Irish Legion. The "promises" referred to here were for substantial pay and promotions to be made to the Irish Legion upon their arrival in Venezuela.
3 "9o" refers to the ninth year of the revolution, dating from the Declaration of Independence in 1810.

22

LETTER TO THOMAS COCHRANE

23 August 1821

Naval strategy is an understudied aspect of the Gran Colombian Wars of Independence, with interest predictably focusing on the big terrestrial battles. Bolívar was aware, however, that naval capacity was essential to repelling Spanish invasions. He assured Venezuela's naval security by maintaining the neutrality of Great Britain, the Atlantic's hegemonic naval power in the years after victory at the Battle of Trafalgar (1805). Bolívar still needed a functioning navy in the Caribbean, however, and this was under the control of Admiral Louis Brión until 1821 (see below). That same year the Colombian Army's successful thrusts southwards opened up the Pacific Ocean as a potential field of combat for Colombia. Bolívar had few resources and fewer personnel with experience in the Pacific; for this reason he turned so enthusiastically to the Scottish adventurer and mercenary, Lord Thomas Cochrane, who had transformed the naval fortunes of the republic of Chile in 1818–19.

Dear Admiral Cochrane:[1]

My Lord,

As I come closer to the ancient Empires of the Incas and the nascent republics of the southern hemisphere, one of the greatest satisfactions that awaits me will be to meet you. I long to pay heartfelt tribute in person to you, one of the most illustrious defenders of world freedom.

Yes, My Lord, I will soon be fortunate enough to meet Your Excellency in the very theatre of your recent glories, in the waters of the Pacific.

I urge Your Excellency to exploit your victories and to come to cooperate with us on Colombia's Panamanian Coasts. Come and help us to carry Colombian soldiers south to Peru. They have left their standards in triumph planted on the Republic's walls, and now they wish to fly to the Southern Andes to embrace their intrepid and worthy brothers–in–arms. Together they will march to break apart the chains that still oppress America's sons.

The Chilean Squadron, Lord Cochrane's Squadron, will escort the Colombian Army over the seas which you have freed from commerce's enemies, as they go to aid Peru in its hour of need.

I do not doubt, My Lord, that Your Excellency's magnanimous disposition will lead you to take every measure to quicken your step and help us to annihilate the Evil Empire in the New World forever.

My aide-de-camp Colonel Ibarra will have the honour of delivering this letter to you, and I ask him also to inform you of my most cordial greetings and the consideration and respect I feel for Your Excellency. He will also be the organ for any future communications that you will be so good as to receive.

With the greatest consideration for Your Excellency, I am your most attentive and obedient servant,

Simón Bolívar
Trujillo, 23 August 1821

NOTE

1 The best biography of the controversial Cochrane is Robert Harvey, *Cochrane: The Life and Exploits of a Fighting Captain*, London, 2002. In the event Cochrane passed only fleetingly through the Colombian service and so was not able to emulate his own heroics from the independence of Chile. Peruvian ships did, however, eventually contribute to the transport south of Colombian soldiers from Panama. Cochrane subsequently went on to achieve further fame and notoriety in Brazil, Greece and the British House of Lords.

23

LETTER TO WILLIAM PARKER

12 December 1821

The Curacao-born Admiral Louis Brión, whose death this letter concerns, was one of the principal instigators of Venezuelan naval mobilization during the Wars of Independence. He had been imprisoned several times by the British during the Napoleonic Wars. He developed a trusting relationship with Bolívar, who was always been happy to defer to Brión's experience on naval matters. Brión's death from tuberculosis left Bolívar increasingly dependent on the naval capabilities of his British and Irish mercenaries—against whom Brion had fought before joining Bolívar's forces. During Brión's lifetime the island of Curacao was much sought after and fought over by Spain, Britain, France and the Netherlands. In addition to Brión, one other native of Curacao played an important role in Venezuelan Independence: Manuel Piar (see Document 8).

To William Parker:

My dear Sir,
I have received with great pain the honourable message which you sent me with Mr Santana. The news of the death of His Excellency Admiral Brión has filled me with the deepest pain.[1] Our first colleague in the noble endeavour to bring about Colombia's freedom is no more! But Colombia owes him at least half of its current fortune, and he was deserving of every reward.

He was a singular man who loved humanity and the citizens of his adopted country more than his own fortune. He risked everything in order to satisfy his noble feelings and to sate his thirst for Glory. In every Colombian heart there will be an altar dedicated to the gratitude we owe the Admiral.

I will be the first to erect eternal monuments in memory of the good that he did for my patria, and in honour of his magnanimous character, which will record his efforts for the most remote posterity. The sublime memory of Admiral Brión's liberality will live on forever. It will be our sacred obligation to fulfil his last wishes. Our benefactor's family will receive preferential treatment whenever they wish; none deserve it more than them.

The Executive Power will be charged with dealing with the Admiral's debtors, and as soon as I return from Quito I will do everything I can to liquidate all debts owed to him as soon as possible.

Sir, please pass on to the late Admiral's daughters my most sincere expressions of best wishes. Please pass on to them the purity of my message of respect and the depth of the irreparable loss that I feel.

I have the honour of offering you, Sir, the most respectful consideration, and I am

Your attentive servant,

Simón Bolívar
Bogotá, 12 December 1821

NOTE

1 There is no biography yet of Brión in English; a good one in Spanish is Johannes Hartog, *Biografía del almirante Luis Brión* (Caracas: Academia Nacional de la Historia, 1983).

24

INVITING GOVERNMENTS TO A CONGRESS IN PANAMA

7 December 1824

Ever since the "Jamaica Letter" (1815) Bolívar had dreamt of greater Spanish American unity; not as one nation but as a federation or league of Spanish American nations. In late 1824, he resolved to put his dream into action, writing this invitation to Hispanic American republics to meet at a Congress in Panama. He excluded Brazil on the grounds that it was a monarchy, and Haiti and the United States because of their different languages, histories and cultures. Although its impact was limited in the 1820s, Bolívar's Congress of Panama is held to be the forerunner of all present-day projects for Latin American unity.

His Excellency The Liberator of Colombia and Supreme Commander of the Republic of Peru, extending an invitation to the Governments of the other Republics of America, to send Representatives to Panama for the purpose of holding a General Assembly there.

My great and good friend,

After fifteen years of sacrifices devoted to the struggle for American freedom, it is time to secure a system of guarantees that will shield our new destiny in both peace and war.[1] The interests and ties that already unite the American republics that were formerly Spanish colonies should be given a fundamental basis that will perpetuate, if possible, the duration of these governments.[2]

A sublime authority is needed to initiate that system, and to concentrate the power of this great political body. This authority must be able to direct our governments' policies, its influence should ensure uniformity of principles, and its very name should put an end to our quarrels.

Such a respected authority can exist only in an assembly of plenipotentiaries appointed by each of our Republics and convened under the auspices of the victory obtained by our arms over Spanish power.[3]

Profoundly persuaded of the importance of these ideas, in 1822 as President of the Republic of Colombia I invited the governments of Mexico, Peru, Chile and Buenos Aires to form a confederation and to convene at the isthmus of Panama, or at some other point agreed upon by the majority, a congress of plenipotentiaries from each state "that should act as a council during periods of great conflicts, to be appealed to in the event of common danger, and to be a faithful interpreter of public treaties when difficulties arise, in brief, to conciliate all our differences."

On June 6 of that year, the government of Peru concluded a treaty of alliance and confederation with the Colombian plenipotentiaries. By said treaty both parties bound themselves to interpose their good offices with the governments of America formerly Spanish, so that, after all had entered into the same agreement, the General Congress of the confederates could be held. A similar treaty was concluded with Mexico on 3 October 1823 by the Colombian envoy to that country, and there are strong reasons for hoping that Mexico will adopt a similar policy in line with the wisdom of their own best interests.

To defer any longer the meeting of the General Congress of the plenipotentiaries of the Republics that, in fact, are already allied, in order to await the decision of the others would be to deprive ourselves of the advantages which that assembly will afford from its very beginning.

The number of these advantages is considerably increased when we but contemplate the spectacle presented to us by the political world, particularly the European continent.

A gathering of the plenipotentiaries of Mexico, Colombia, and Peru will be indefinitely delayed, unless it is instigated by one of these contracting parties, or unless the time and place for the carrying out of this great plan are determined in a preliminary convention.

In view of the difficulties and delays that are presented by the distance separating us, together with other grave motives that general interests suggest, I have decided to take this step with a view toward bringing about an immediate meeting of our plenipotentiaries, while the other governments are completing the necessary preliminaries, already concluded by us, concerning the appointment and commissioning of their representatives.

With respect to the opening date of the Congress, I make so bold as to suggest that no obstacle can oppose its convening within six months from this very date; and I shall also go so far as to flatter myself that the ardent desire which stirs every American to exalt the power of the world of Columbus will overcome the obstacles and delays demanded by ministerial preparations and the distance separating the capital of each State from the central point of the meeting. It seems that, if the whole world should have to choose its capital, the isthmus of Panama, located as it is in the center of the globe, with Asia on one side and Africa and Europe on the other, would be the site chosen for this grand design. The isthmus of Panama has been offered for this purpose in the existing treaties by the Colombian government. The isthmus is equidistant from the extremities of the continent, and for this reason it ought to be the provisional location for the first meeting of the confederates.

I myself have yielded to these considerations, and I am seriously disposed toward sending to Panama the delegates from this Republic immediately upon my being honoured with the desired reply to this circular letter. Indeed, nothing can so satisfy the ardent desire of my heart as a general agreement on the part of the confederated governments to accomplish this solemn American act.

Major delays and difficulties will result if Your Excellency should not participate in this plan, at a time when the momentum of world events speeds everything on, an acceleration which may not be to our benefit.

Once the first conferences between the plenipotentiaries are held, the permanent seat of the Congress, as well as its powers, can be solemnly agreed upon by the majority, and then all our hopes will have been realized.

The day when our plenipotentiaries exchange their credentials will mark an immortal epoch in the diplomatic history of the world.

A hundred years from now, when historians trace the origins of our public laws, and they recall the treaties that consolidated its destiny, they will look with awe upon the protocols of the isthmus. There they will find the outlines of our first alliances, which will trace the progress of our relations with the rest of the world. How the isthmus of Corinth will then pale in comparison with that of Panama![4]

Your great and good friend,

Simón Bolívar
Lima, 7 December 1824

Minister of Foreign Relations, José Sánchez Carrión.

NOTES

1 Translation by Lewis Bertrand with revisions by Matthew Brown. Bertrand's version is excellent on the central section, though I have made substantial changes to style and format elsewhere.

2 The confluence in timing should be noted between the writing of this invitation (in Lima, on 7 December 1824) and the final battle of Peruvian and South American independence (at Ayacucho, on 9 December 1824).

3 Bolívar eventually also invited representatives of the United States and Great Britain to the Congress, though for various reasons their presence and influence were minimal. For a good discussion of the geopolitical context of the Congress of Panama see Juan Diego Jaramillo, *Bolívar y Canning 1822–1827: Desde el congreso de Verona hasta el congreso de Panamá* (Bogotá: Banco de la República, 1983). The Congress itself was poorly attended and ineffectual, for reasons explained in Lynch, *Simón Bolívar,* pp.213–4.

4 In my revision here, I have borrowed Frederick Fornoff's usage of the phrase "pale in comparison" in his translation for OUP.

25

LETTER TO GENERAL LAFAYETTE

20 March 1826

From the mid-1820s onward, Bolívar was especially conscious of assuring his place in history as a great figure in South American Independence. He rebutted comparisons with figures he disapproved of (such as Napoleon Bonaparte) and accepted those he felt honoured by (such as George Washington). In the 1820s, one of the most popular ways of expressing tribute or praise to republican heroes was by commissioning and sending portraits or personal effects as gifts, which is something that Bolívar did in the scenario he describes here. If one wished to go even further, one could send cuttings of the subjects' hair (though this is not the case here), and it is for this reason that locks of Bolívar's hair can today be found around the world, from Caracas and Bogotá to Ipswich (England) and Paris.

Dear General Lafayette,

I have had the honour to see, for the first time, the noble profile of the man who did so much good for the New World. I owe this pleasure to Colonel Mercier, who has delivered to me your letter dated 15 October last year [1825]. I have learnt from the public papers that you have been so kind as to honour me with a treasure from Mount Vernon. This has produced in me an unexplainable joy.

The portrait of Washington, some mementos, and one of the monuments of his Glory, are to be given unto me by your hands, in the name of the brothers of the Great Citizen, the first born son of the New World.

I am unable to find the words to explain the emotions welling up in my heart at this moment. Your high regard is a great glory for me. Washington's family honours me more than I would have dared hope or imagine, because Washington presented by Lafayette must be the crown of all human rewards.

Washington was the noble protector of social reforms, and you are the Citizen Hero, the Athlete of Liberty, who served America with one hand and Europe with the other. Oh! What mortal could possibly deserve the honours which you thrust upon me? I do not know what to say; the honour I feel is immense. I offer you all the respect and veneration which you deserve as the Titan of freedom.

With great consideration I am your respectful admirer.

Simón Bolívar
Lima, 20 March 1826